Froude Today

Froude Today

John Coleman

NEW EUROPEAN PUBLICATIONS LONDON

Published in the United Kingdom in 2005 by

New European Publication
14-16 Carroun Road
London SW8 1JT, England

British Library Cataloguing in Publication Data

ISBN 1 872410-38-3

Cover design & layout: orbitgraphic.co.uk

Printed and bound in Great Britain by Antony Rowe, Chippenham, Wiltshire.

Contents

Acknowledgments

Writing is a lonely business and so the help of several people has made it less so. Sir Richard Body not only suggested the simple title thus avoiding such awkward phrases as 'relevant to the present' etc. but also read through the whole text and made a host of valuable suggestions. Aidan Rankin kept the watchful eye of editor on it as it developed. Helen Carroll did much more than proof read the script. She reinforced some of the other criticisms, in particular that Froude's Study on Calvinism should not be in the main text but in an appendix, as well as adding some very useful suggestions of her own. I am also very grateful to orbitgraphic for their patience and helpfulness as typesetters in getting the whole thing in the shape of a book.

And my final thanks to Professor David Rankin for translating and checking the Greek quotations.

'And I rejoice very much to see Mr. Froude's face here, with all our added acquaintance with him in his books. His History is well-known, I know, to all good readers in this country, and he has established the importance of his own opinion, of his own judgement, in these books. I think he has taught us much. He has shown at least two eminent faculties in his histories – the faculty of seeing wholes, and the faculty of seeing and saying particulars. The one makes history valuable, and the other makes it readable – interesting. Both these qualities his writings have eminently shown. I think we are indebted to him for a power which is imminent in them, the discretion which is given us; the speeches, the language of the very persons whom his history records. The language, the style of the books, draws very much of its excellence from that habit, that practice, of giving the very language of the times. He knows well that old English people and Irish people of whom his history records the events did not write or speak in the style of the Edinburgh Review or the North American Review, but that they spoke a stern and dreadful language, when words were few and when words meant much. So that the language is like the cry of the soldier when the battle begins, or the cry of the fugitive when the battle turns against him. It is a pithy and wonderful language. If you remember, it is Shakespeare that says, 'When breath is scant, it's very seldom spent in vain'.'

R.W. Emerson
Welcoming Speech, New York, 1872.

'Duty changes, truth expands, one age cannot teach another either the details of its obligations or the matter of its knowledge, but the principle of obligation is everlasting.'

James Anthony Froude

'The world would be most happily governed if it consisted not of a few aggregations secured by wars of conquest, with their accompaniments of despotism and tyrannic rule, but of a society of small states living together in amity, not transgressing each other's limits, unbroken by jealousies,'

St. Augustine of Hippo

Chapter 1

Introduction

In defending Thomas Carlyle against the charge that he preached the doctrine of Might is Right, Froude retorted that the truth was the exact reverse: that Right is Might. This is the lesson of the story of David and Goliath and it is a lesson that needs to be preached in every age. The people, the institutions and the organisations which we imagine to be all powerful are often the ones that collapse most rapidly when faced with the still small voice of Truth. Napoleon once said that there were two forces that could be used to control mankind, fear and love, and he gave Jesus Christ as an example of the latter and his own failure as an example of the former. The belief that Right in the end has the power to defeat Might against all odds is the indisputable source of Hope for humanity. It shines through all of Froude's writing and I believe is needed more today than in his own time.

The adult life of James Anthony Froude almost exactly spanned the Victorian era. He was born in 1818 and lived until 1894. He achieved great contemporary fame as the historian who revised the prevailing assessment of the Tudor period and in particular the reputation of Henry VIII by unearthing the documents and exposing the dangers that threatened England. Understanding the Spanish threat, with its subtle penetration of

English public life through spies, intrigues and overwhelming military force, in many ways not unlike the threat of the Soviet Union in the Cold War, but cloaked in Roman Catholic dress, was the purpose of his extensive research in Spain. His history caused much controversy which has lasted down to the present day, but that is not the subject of this book. Here I am concerned with his attitude to the politics of his own times, a matter on which he had clear ideas. In fact Gladstone, when introducing his Irish Home Rule Bill in Parliament and quoting at length from Froude's history of Ireland, referred to him as 'perhaps a man of prepossessions – on that I give no opinion – is certainly a man of truth and honour who, if he sees what he believes to be injustice, will not allow his heart and his conscience to tamper with the principles involved in exposing it'. Many attempts had been made to induce him to come into Parliament and in a host of ways his resolute refusal is what makes him so interesting today. 'Politicians,' he said, 'were like men who, having been given two eyes by nature, deliberately extinguish one'.

Froude was sometimes referred to as the 'darling' of the British Empire and yet I believe he would have agreed with that arch enemy of British imperialism, Thomas Jefferson, when he said, 'Whenever a man has cast a longing eye on them (offices of government), a rottenness begins in his conduct'. These two points, his view of Empire and his worries about the voting aspects of democracy are the main reasons for looking at what he has to say. He saw the roots of the problems which the world is struggling with today. He saw the Empire as he describes it in *Oceana*[1] as a network of human communities hanging together and having their own roots, not as an organization with London as its centre, as his robust criticisms of the Colonial Office imply. Understood in this way it was also a template for global peace and stability. He saw democracy as a system of vote catching that would lead to disaster and yet his American friend Bret Harte was able to say that at the very core of his thinking the spirit rather than the letter of democracy was always present. At a time when cynicism is the dominant aspect in the Western World towards political representatives, Froude points the way to regaining trust in these days when pluralistic democracy is almost synonymous with non-violent civil war, and the market is seen as the ultimate defining factor of political life, something Aidan Rankin has called 'market fundamentalism' in his book, *The Politics of the Forked Tongue*.[2]

A few words about Froude's childhood may help to explain what some may see as the severity of his outlook. His mother died when he was two and was too ill in the brief years before her death to give him the attention an infant needs. His father was an archdeacon in the Church of England and felt that his sons should follow the traditional careers open to gentlemen. His brother, Hurrel, was harsh towards him and felt he should do all in his power to make a man of him. Hurrel died young and death seemed an ever present prospect during Froude's childhood and early youth. No doubt this played its part in the vividness that developed in his writing. The thought of imminent death does give an acuteness to our thinking.

The vividness of Froude's writing is hard, if not impossible to match and that is my excuse for the very generous use of quotations in this book. Palgrave considered Froude's prose at its best the finest in the nineteenth century. My aim is to present Froude to today's reader and so wherever appropriate I shall use his own words in preference to an inferior substitute of my own. His attitude to America is almost certainly the one that should engage us most today and that was inextricably linked to his ideas about the British Empire.

My hope is that this will be a book not just for readers of one political persuasion but for all and even for those of no persuasion at all. In Victorian England, James Anthony Froude – to his friends Anthony Froude – stood significantly apart from the political system and yet had a vast influence upon it. For that very reason we may look upon his ideas as standing outside any particular historical period and therefore relevant to today, sometimes strangely so. *Oceana* in particular influenced the first part of the 20th century, certainly until the end of the Second World War. The Empire became a major theme in British life. Schoolchildren were shown the extensive pink parts on the map of the world and told to be proud of them and be ready to serve the Empire. Every year an Empire day was celebrated; and yet it was hardly what Froude advocated when his vision is examined closely. The Second World War signalled the end of the British Empire. President Roosevelt in particular was anxious to sweep away the old attitude of Empire and replace it with something more modern and less class-ridden and stick-in-the-mud. He once said that when the war was over he would 'break up the British Empire and attach the pieces to the trading blocks of the world'.

The questions which this book confronts principally are whether what is supposed to replace the British Empire is really any better and secondly ask whether the Empire in Froude's sense has really completely disappeared? In a host of ways the Commonwealth may be moving nearer to what Froude would have seen as his dream. Of course it seems to lack power and influence in a world which is – if it is not already quite there – travelling in the direction of 'the Might is Right' way of ordering human affairs. President Eisenhower complained towards the end of his life that during his time as a soldier and as President he had watched the growth of 'the unwarranted influence of a military-industrial complex' and that it would lead to a 'disastrous misplacement of power'. This of course applied not just to America but to the Western world generally.

One of the aspects of Froude's thinking which I wish to lay the utmost stress upon in this book is that his concept of Empire never rested on a power foundation. It was in fact a negation of what we normally think of as centralised political power. The Commonwealth, though regarded as weak in that sense, still even in this present age is comprised of many of the most significant elements of *Oceana*. It has been through the fire of post-World War Two political turmoil, has a hidden strength and perhaps holds the clue to building a better world. A few years ago Chief Emeka Anyaoku, the Commonwealth Secretary-General, wrote an article in the journal *New European*[3] entitled, 'Europe or the Commonwealth: A False Dichotomy'. He certainly had no doubt about the importance of the Commonwealth and the principle on which it is based: '... it also provides a window on the world, a panorama embracing one quarter of the world's people, one third of the world's sovereign nations...' Churchill also knew the importance of the British Commonwealth – as Victor Montagu once told me, 'in my day we were all brought up on Froude'. Montagu, despite his title of Earl of Sandwich, chose to serve in the House of Commons and was a close associate of Stanley Baldwin, the Conservative party leader. Sir John Biggs-Davidson, who worked closely with Churchill in the immediate post-war days, said in 'The Two Commonwealths'[4] – another *New European* article – that Churchill wanted to see the British Commonwealth as a whole moved into place and linked with a great European Commonwealth. 'There should not,' he wrote, 'have been a Treaty of Rome in 1957. There should have been a Treaty of London in 1947'. Both Commonwealths would have been composed of sovereign nations willingly bound by agreement to co-operate. The British leaders of the first half of the 20th century grew up not only under the influence of Froude on the one hand, but of Victorian Liberalism on the other. The two did not mix easily. The 20th century led us along a hard, bitter and bloody road – and although the sense of duty perhaps led directly to the over-harsh attitudes of the military leaders of the First World War, it was wildly out of context – but we may now ask the question: didn't it take us to the present point at which Froude's dream could begin to be implemented?

This book will be divided into three distinct parts. The first is this introduction, which will include an article I wrote on Froude for the *Salisbury Review*.[5] It is a broad introduction to Froude's thinking which is the core of the book. Those who want to study his historical works should read the books themselves. Those who want to know more about his life should read Professor Dunn's biography,[6] which had the advantage of access to the collection of biographical notes and letters kept by his daughter Margaret Froude. It would be hard to imagine a better account than that contained in its two volumes. The four chapters which follow this will deal with education, religion and politics and will include many long passages from Froude himself. The penultimate chapter will rely, I hope, on reasonably informed imagination. I want to venture on to territory that angels might be wary of tiptoeing over, and imagine that Froude has been watching over us from above for the past hundred years or so and that he has come back to comment on the times since he was alive and on events today, as well as a few predications for the future. Inadequate as this may be it may yet be hoped that it will be enough to stimulate the thoughts of readers to get a true grasp of Froude today and in fact to get a better grasp of today. At least they will be able to use the preceding chapters to see how it squares with Froude's writings about his own times. The final chapter contains some thoughts of my own.

In 2002, I wrote the article for that most conservative of journals, *The Salisbury Review*, entitled 'James Anthony Froude and the Roots of our Modern Political Malaise', because I felt it was time that the Conservative Party took a new look at its own history and thought more clearly about where it should be in the current political situation. Needless to say the Labour Party needs to do the same. I found it both amusing and significant that Lord Hattersley recently commented: 'The Labour Party once reflected the best prejudices of the British working class; now it reflects the worst'. It seemed to me that the article I wrote was a skeleton on which I wanted to put much more flesh. Hence this book, but as a skeleton it would be very appropriate as the main part of this introduction and since it begins with a letter from the Marquess of Salisbury whom, incidentally, Clement Attlee considered the best Prime Minister of the 19th Century, it may be thought of as applying to both the left and the right.

The article, 'James Anthony Froude and the Roots of our Modern Political Malaise', which led to the writing of this book, follows below.

*

In writing about James Anthony Froude in this journal it is surely most appropriate to begin with the letter from Lord Salisbury in 1892 offering him the Regius Professorship of Modern History at Oxford, two years before his death:

Dear Mr Froude,

*As you are doubtless aware, the Regius Professorship of Modern History at Oxford is vacant by Dr Freeman's death. I write to you with some hesitation: for on the one hand it may be that you are thoroughly disinclined for the duties of such a post – though they are not heavy. On the other hand, I do not like to sacrifice any chance of obtaining the services for Oxford of her most famous historian – a feeling to which a recent perusal of **Katharine of Aragon** has naturally given great vividness. Pardon me if I have done wrong in asking you to allow me to submit your name to the Queen.[7]*

In any case consider this communication confidential for the present.

Yours very truly,

Salisbury

Froude had had difficult times at Oxford after the publication of *Nemesis of Faith* in 1849. Like his friend John Ruskin he was unhappy with the popular Victorian version of religion, which Ruskin described as 'gas lighted, gas inspired Christianity'. He was also viciously attacked, as Lord Salisbury must have known, by his predecessor as Professor of Modern History, Edward Freeman, whose taunt that he was 'constitutionally inaccurate' has pursued him ever since and is even to be found in recent editions of the *Encyclopaedia Britannica*. His American biographer Waldo Hilary Dunn has done much to restore his reputation as a historian. The second volume of the biography starts with a quotation from Professor Francis Clarke in the *London Mercury* of August 1930:

> If his "constitutional inaccuracy" is to remain a compulsory article in the creed of historical scholars, it is time some constitutionally accurate scholar began to prove it.

The motivation perhaps for much of the opposition to Froude has its origins in the emerging scientific spirit of the Victorian era. His essay 'The Science of History' expressed his view that it is hard to verify a fact in the present day, never mind five hundred years earlier. The accuracy of his painstaking historical works as opposed to certain articles and sketches is probably beyond question, but his view of history that it is nearer to a drama than a chronicle is disturbing to historians.

The third major conflict in his life was with the political economists of his time, those who argued that everything is determined by market forces and that morality is only applicable at the individual level. His view of the economists is clearly expressed in his biography of Disraeli, whose views on this subject he saw as identical to his own:

> Under the old organisation of England, the different orders of men were bound together under reciprocal obligations of duty. The economists and their political followers held that duty had nothing to do with it. Food, wages, and all else had their market value, which could be interfered with only to the general injury. The employer was to hire his labourers or his hands at the lowest rate at which they could be induced to work. If he ceased to need them, or if they would not work on terms which would remunerate him, he was at liberty to turn them off. The labourers, in return, might make the best of their own opportunity and sell their services to the best advantage which competition allowed. The capitalists found the arrangement satisfactory to them. The people found it less satisfactory, and they replied by Chartism and rick-burnings.[8]

Froude wanted both sides regulated by duty. 'Liberty in the modern sense,' he wrote, 'liberty where the rights of man take the place of the duties of man – such a liberty they [the old English] neither sought nor desired'. This idea is expanded on vividly (to borrow Lord Salisbury's word about *Katharine of Aragon*) in his the chapter on 'England and Her Colonies' in his *Short Studies on Great Subjects:*

> Under the conditions which I have supposed, England would become, still more than it is at present, a country of enormous cities. The industry on which its prosperity would depend can only be carried on when large masses of people are congregated together, and the tendency already visible towards a diminution of her agricultural population would become increasingly active. Large estates are fast devouring small estates; large farms, small

farms ... I have spoken of the effect of modern city life upon the body: it would be easy were it likely to be of any service to say more of its effect upon the mind. In those past generations, when the English character was moulding itself, there was a virtue specially recognized among us called content. We were a people who lived much by custom. ... The same family continued in the same farm, neither adding to its acres nor diminishing them. Shop, factory and warehouse were handed down with the same stationary character, yielding constant but moderate profits, to which the habits of life were adjusted. Satisfied with his share of this world's goods which his situation in life assigned to him, the tradesman aspired no higher, endeavouring only in the words of the antiquated catechism 'to do his duty in that state of life to which it pleased God to call him'. Throughout the country there was an ordered, moderate, and temperate contentedness, energetic – but energetic more in doing well the work that was to be done, than in 'bettering' this or that person's position in life. Something of this lingers yet among old-fashioned people in holes and corners of England; but it is alien both to the principles and the temper of the new era. To push on, to climb vigorously on the slippery steps of the social ladder, to raise ourselves one step or more out of the rank of life in which we were born, is now converted into a duty. It is the condition under which each of us plays his proper part as a factor in the general progress. The more commercial prosperity increases, the more universal such a habit of mind becomes. It is the first element of success in the course to which the country seems to be committing itself. There must be no rest, no standing still, no pausing to take breath. The stability of such a system depends, like the boy's top, on the rapidity of its speed. To stop is to fall; to slacken speed is to be overtaken by our rivals. We are whirled along in the breathless race of competition. The motion becomes faster and faster, and the man must be unlike anything which the experience of humanity gives us a right to hope for, who can retain his conscience, or any one of the nobler qualities, in so wild a career.[9]

Is such a state of things a wholesome one? Is it politically safe? Is it morally tolerable? Is it not certain for one thing that a competition, of which profit is the first object, will breed dishonesty as carrion breeds worms?

In his day Froude could look towards America with hope, great hope. He wrote:

They are the people of the future. In the Americans we may read the character and tendencies of the ages that are to be. They are sprung, like us, from the loins of our own fathers. They claim an equal share with us in the traditions of English history; and their great men trace their descent with as much pride from historical families. Theirs as well as ours are the Plantagenet and Tudor princes. Theirs are Drake and Raleigh, Burghley and Cromwell. Theirs are Chaucer and Shakespeare and Bunyan. In our modern poets and men of science, in Scott and Byron, in Burns and Tennyson, in Macaulay and Carlyle, in Tyndal, in Huxley, in Darwin, in John Mill, they will allow us no exclusive right of possession. Let any Englishman, whom the Americans have learnt to respect, go over there among them and see if he is received as a stranger. Their voluntary and instinctive sympathies prove that between the American and English peoples there are bonds uniting them closer than those which unite any nations on the globe, and only the action of what are called the governing classes among us prevents the political relations from becoming as intimate as the spiritual.[10]

If Froude were alive today, I think he would have been very sad to see the Victorian commercial culture which he so heartily disliked dominating the United States of America and extended to include the selling of ideas and even selling one's own person, not just one's labour. He would also have been sad to see England's involvement in the present structures of Continental Europe at the expense of both Commonwealth and American links, although I believe he would have welcomed the efforts to construct more peaceful relationships between the Continental nations. He quoted Washington's famous remarks in 1791 about keeping America clear of the entanglements of war, preparation for war and the commotions in Europe and England. Even now I think he would have suspected that many of the old rivalries and quarrels were not so far below the surface. He thought the only sound basis for federation was mutual goodwill, not the scheming of the so-called governing classes.

His views on the two most notable Prime Ministers of the Victorian period, Gladstone and Disraeli, and theirs on him, can only be touched on here. He strongly disliked what he feared would be the effect of Liberal policies and was certainly not well disposed towards Gladstone, believing that he had little sense of the thoughts and feelings of ordinary people. When Disraeli came into a dinner one sensed a response from everyone present, from the Queen to the waiters. Nevertheless he was surprised and pleased when Gladstone responded favourably to his biography of Disraeli. For although he certainly may have disagreed with many of Froude's views, Gladstone had a very high regard for him as he showed by quoting from *The English in Ireland* at length in introducing the Home Rule Bill in Parliament.

Froude's view of Disraeli was quite another matter, although he disliked some of his more jingoistic policies with a remarkable intensity. In preparing to write the biography – and he hesitated about this and perhaps would not have done it without the help of Ralph Disraeli, the Prime Minister's brother – he revealed his motivation in a letter to Lady Derby: 'The point is to make out what there was behind the mask. Had it not been for *Lothair* I should have said nothing but a charlatan. But that altered my opinion, and the more often I read it the more I want to know what his real nature was.'[11]

Froude was surprised and I suspect pleased at Gladstone's positive response to the book.

A few of his thoughts about Empire must be included here. He was no imperialist centralizer. I am sure he would have welcomed the term Commonwealth. He wrote:

No province of such an Empire will be denuded of its wealth, denuded of its genius, denuded of its self-dependence, where the life-blood of the heart will flow freely to the furthest extremities. I saw in Natal a colossal fig tree. It had a central stem, but I knew not where the centre was, for the branches bent to the ground and struck root there; and at each point a fresh trunk shot up erect, and threw out new branches in turn, which again arched and planted themselves till the single tree had become a forest, and overhead was spread a vast dome of leaves and fruit, which was supported on innumerable columns, like the roof of some vast cathedral. I saw an image as I looked at it, of the future of England and her colonies, if the English people can read the signs of the times.[12]

No doubt Froude would have been delighted today if he could see a similar structure arising in Europe in peace and partnership. Indeed he wished that to happen for the common good of all mankind and yet he knew that there was a cancer latent in most political – indeed most human – endeavours that can suddenly and tragically spring to life. The demon of ambition, that drive always to push ahead and never to be content with the position in life in which we find ourselves, could and did ruin the chances of such a hope coming to fruition in this present world.

Many Liberals might have considered Froude an absolutist, but a wiser estimate was expressed by the American Bret Harte in a letter to his wife when he was staying with the Froudes in Devon: 'He is great, honest, manly – democratic in the best sense of word.' Froude was never too sanguine about his hopes for the future and his mixed feelings come vividly through another letter to Lady Derby in 1880:

> I am glad there is to be an end to "glory and gunpowder", but my feelings about Gladstone remain where they were. When you came to power in 1874, I dreamed of a revival of real Conservatism which under wiser guiding might and would have lasted to the end of the century. This is gone – gone for ever. The old England of order and rational government is past and will not return. Now I should like to see a moderate triumvirate – Lord Hartington, Lord Grenville, and your husband, with a Cabinet which they could control. This too may easily be among the impossibilities, but I am sure that at the bottom of its heart the country wants quiet, and a Liberal revolutionary sensationalism will be just as distasteful to reasonable people as "Asian Mysteries", tall talk and ambitious buffooneries.[13]

Much earlier he had written: 'I have no hope that things will go right or that men will think reasonably until they have exhausted every mode of human folly'. His forebodings grew rather than diminished with the years and were similar to those expressed by the Third Marquess of Salisbury when he contemplated the 20th century as he walked along the beach with his daughter as recorded by his most recent biographer Andrew Roberts.[14]

As a postscript it might well be asked what the relevance of these views is today. Froude was not first and foremost an historian. I believe his primary concern was with what was happening in his own times, which his depth of interest in Carlyle amply demonstrates. Were he alive today, I am certain that he would apply the same critical criteria to the present as he did to the Victorian era. It seems to me that in what is now called the post-industrial age, with its intellectual quicksands of post-modernism, the present Conservative Party has nowhere else to turn except to Conservatism in the very sense in which Froude understood it.

The race to which Victorian England was committing itself in his day – which I suppose is what ordinary people now refer to as the 'rat race' – has provided the Labour Party and the Liberals (in all their varieties) with the opportunity to recover every item of clothing stolen from them by the Conservatives over the last 150 years. This competitive society has spawned an education system which is seen by most parents as a means of enabling their children to rise in the volatile social scheme of things. It is the very reverse of the older order which said 'Like father, like son'. John Ruskin described it unforgettably in *Sesame and Lilies*: But, an education "which shall keep a good coat on my son's back; – which shall enable him to ring with confidence the visitors' bell at double-belled doors; which shall result ultimately in the establishment of a double-belled door to his own house; in a word, which shall lead to advancement in life; – this we pray for on bent knees – and this is all we pray for."[15]

However, far from lifting the poor of the world out of destitution, industrial policies based on competition are plunging us into a consumerist nightmare. Neighbours do not co-operate but seek to get one up on each other, the environment is sacrificed to economic growth, those who fail in the 'rat race' resort to street crime, families and communities break down and welfare schemes are largely devised to mitigate the worst effects of the breathless race. Added to this is the fact that those who gain power have to struggle frenetically to manipulate the resentments of the various groups, usually minorities, that they claim to support in order to keep ahead in the opinion polls on which their precarious power depends. Modern sleaze is surely a natural outcome of this race to which the England of Froude's day committed us. Likewise, the negative aspects of feminism are a very understandable response of women who have been bewitched by the spell that has long gripped the world of men.

The war against terrorism, which is substantially a by-product of this competition and cannot really be won, is likely to confront us with the fact that we are at the end of the road on which the Victorians were enthusiastically embarking in Froude's day. Perhaps it will dawn upon mankind that the real choice is whether we build our society on the rock of duty or on the shifting sands of economics.

Froude, like Disraeli, believed that the influential classes had largely jettisoned their obligations to society. Both, however, thought that the working classes had on the whole retained their sense of duty. In the 20th century the trades union leaders looked at the behaviour of their masters, saw the opportunity to exploit it and in doing so created their own greasy pole, not infrequently receiving peerages at the end of their careers. Margaret Thatcher dealt with them in a robust way but failed to deal with the burgeoning forces of corporatism in big business which have blighted the latter half of the twentieth century and now threaten the future at least as much as terrorism.

I believe that both Froude and Lord Salisbury would have dealt with big business and the unions in a more even-handed way, for both men believed in a rational, stable form of government.

*

My problem with this article is that it might appear to be directed at Conservatives whereas in reality I was convinced that Froude provided a framework in which all political debate could take place. Without some clear and firm idea of what we aim to achieve through a civilised political system, that system itself will in the end disintegrate into the worst forms of anarchy and the distrust and disillusionment of the people and eventually turn into civil war, either open or covert.

The England of the 17th and 18th centuries is the place and the period to which Froude so often alluded as the cradle of rational government and to which Voltaire, though French, referred to so admiringly in *Letters on the English*. Rome, he wrote, never achieved that peak of civilisation which England developed, whose princes could rule without arrogance and thus without the thirst for power that the continental aristocracies never entirely escaped and which has generated most of the tragedies of European history. Froude was acutely aware that his own century was leaving all that behind for a course that few politicians in his time, with the exception of Disraeli, could imagine where it would end.

Chapter 2
Education

A general survey of Froude's views might suggest that since he believed that the course the country had embarked upon caused him to feel that the education of his day was highly unsatisfactory, that his view of it might have been similar to Ruskin's. Indeed it was. However his most interesting account of his own views is most clearly expressed in his address to the students of St Andrew's University in 1869 when he was elected Rector. Characteristically he bent over backwards to get as near as possible to understanding the outlook of the young students he was addressing on the verge of their careers in a world even then full of multiplying complexities, without ever fundamentally compromising his own convictions. Two things need to be borne in mind as the background to his own experience: his *Nemesis of Faith* had been publicly burnt in Oxford and he had been excluded from the University after having been a fellow of Oriel College; and secondly his own view of religion indicated in his description of the stationary character of 'old England' in the Short Study already quoted.

Froude's ideas on education are inseparable from and underlie all his thinking and it therefore seems entirely appropriate to begin with education. In his lecture in Scotland he begins with a story designed to appeal to, and challenge the

Scottish students. Almost as an aside he recounts the following story:

> Many years ago, when I was first studying the history of the Reformation in Scotland, I read a story of a slave in a French galley who was one morning bending wearily over his oar. The day was breaking, and, rising out of the grey waters a line of cliffs was visible, and the white houses of a town and a church tower. The rower was a man unused to such service, worn with toil and watching, and likely, it was thought, to die. A companion touched him, pointed to the shore, and asked him if he knew it.[1]
>
> 'Yes,' he answered, 'I know it well. I see the steeple of that place where God opened my mouth in public to His glory; and I know, how weak soever I now appear, 1 shall not depart out of this life till my tongue glorify His name in the same place.'
>
> Gentlemen, that town was St Andrew's, that galley slave was John Knox; and we know that he came back and did 'glorify God' in this place and others to some purpose.

What better story could he have chosen? And having done so he developed it in his own characteristic way of trying to understand his hearers. These were young men whom he knew would have been influenced by the powerful trends of their day, which flew in the face of what Froude tended to believe. He follows that story with a brief but vivid description of what he believed to be the moral foundation of education, which he deduces from the story itself:

> To make us know our duty and do it, to make us upright in thought and word, is the aim of all instruction which deserves the name, the epitome of all purposes for which education exists. Duty changes, truth expands, one age cannot teach another either the details of its obligations or the matter of its knowledge, but the principle of obligation is everlasting. The consciousness of duty, whatever its origin, is to the moral nature of man what life is in the seed-cells of all organized creatures: the condition of coherence, the elementary force in virtue of which it grows.[2]

This was a lesson that Froude believed John Knox determined to teach in Scotland in the face of terrible corruption on the part of the Catholic Lords who at that time held the power. To reinforce his notion that it is when religion has been corrupted he said the following:

> I am not going to quote any fierce old Calvinist who will be set down as a bigot and a liar. My witness is M. Fontenay, brother of the secretary of Mary Stuart, who was residing here on Mary Stuart's business. The persons of whom he was speaking were the so-called Catholic Lords; and the occasion was in a letter to herself:-
>
> 'The Sirens,' wrote this M. Fontenay, 'which bewitch the lords of this country are money and power. If I preach to them of their duty to the Sovereign – if I talk to them of honour, of justice, of virtue, of the illustrious actions of their forefathers, and of the example which they should themselves bequeath to their posterity – they think me a **fool**. They can talk of these things themselves – talk as well as the best philosophers in Europe. But, when it comes to action, they are like the Athenians, who knew what was good, but would not do it. The misfortune of Scotland is that the noble lords will not look beyond the points of their shoes. They care nothing for the future and less for the past.[3]

Froude's positive though misunderstood attitude to the priests in Ireland, which is considered in the chapter on religion, shows that he did not have a prejudice against Catholicism *per se* but against the corruption that made reformation and revolution necessary, although it is clear from what he writes elsewhere that he fears that if it got back its old political power it might well be tempted into its old ways again.

Froude goes on to point out that everyone admits this in words: 'Rather it has become a cant now-a-days to make a parade of noble intentions'. In our modern world we are inclined to drop even the pretence of good intentions and noble ideals and positively encourage harmful ways of behaviour. In Froude's day he felt there was no uncertainty about the normal occupations – 'are we traders, mechanics, lawyers, doctors – our duty is to do our work as honestly and as well as we can?'

Much is said in this address, as might well be expected, on the qualities of the Scots and an interesting distinction between nature and nurture is brought in. Froude is not in much doubt that the inherited qualities of a people or a society develop over many generations. So after speaking of the qualities that the young men in front of him bring with them into life because of their breeding as Scots, he says, 'and the other part of your equipment is only second in importance to it: I mean your education'. He then makes a comparison very much in favour of the Scottish approach to education: "It is fair all round to rich and poor alike. You have broken down, or you never permitted to rise, the enormous barriers of expense which makes the highest education in England a privilege of the wealthy."[4]

Froude goes on to discuss the subject matter of education, on which he had the strongest views. 'Education,' he continues, 'is on everybody's lips. Our own great schools and colleges are in the middle of a revolution, which like most revolutions, means discontent with what we have, and no clear idea of what we would have.' The causes he adds are not far to seek. 'On the one hand there is an immense multiplication of the subjects of knowledge, through the progress of science and the investigation on all sides into the present and past condition of this planet and its inhabitants; on the other, the equally increased range of occupations among which the working part of mankind are now distributed, and for one or other of which our education is intended to qualify us'. Here he comes on to what is now known as the 'information overload'. Mentioning the classical education of the subjects of the century, he adds: 'Yet if we try to pile on top of these histories and literatures of our own and other nations, with modern languages and sciences, we accumulate a load of matter which the most ardent and industrious student cannot be expected to cope with'.

He then emphasises once again the importance of knowing clearly the kind of result you wish to produce in any activity you undertake. The house-builder doesn't just gather a mass of bricks and timber but works to a clear plan. 'I have long thought that, to educate successfully you should first ascertain clearly, with sharp and distinct outline, what you mean by an educated man'.

We are now coming to the heart of what Froude meant by the fundamentals of education. Here he turns to 'our ancestors'. For 'whatever their shortcomings' he explains, 'they understood perfectly well what they meant. In both their primary and higher education they were clear. They set out with the principle that every child born in this world, (and it must be remembered that Froude himself lived at a time when in England quite a considerable number of children were 'disposed of' every year), should be taught to do his duty to God and man. The majority of people had to live, as they always must, by bodily labour; therefore every boy was as early as possible set to labour. He was not permitted to idle about the streets or lanes. He was apprenticed to some honest industry. Either he was sent to a farm, or, if his wits were sharper, he was allotted to the village carpenter, bricklayer, tailor, shoemaker or whatever it might be'.[5]

Apprenticeship was the normal course for boys and it was regulated by the magistrates and established by law. Indeed even scholars were in effect apprenticed to their tutor in the old universities, but an important distinction was made in the Middle Ages between what had a product at the end of it, and scholarship. Froude laid the very heaviest emphasis upon this. The worker should be rewarded as the value of his work could be fairly easily estimated and he could be paid accordingly. The scholar who produced little has wealth of the mind and should expect little. Spinoza, who despite being offered much insisted on maintaining his independence upon grinding lenses for microscopes and telescopes and, Froude mentions, spoke of the kind of wealth that for one man to possess promoted his neighbour's wealth, rather than detracting from it. Scholars were not to be a burden on the rest of mankind, or as we say today, on the taxpayer. What a difference it would make to the cost of education if that principle were applied. The principle is vividly illustrated by the following passage from his address:

> The thirty thousand students who gathered out of Europe to listen to Abelard did not travel in carriages, and they brought no port-manteaus with them. They carried their wardrobes on their backs. They walked from Paris to Padua, from Padua to Salamanca, and they begged their way along the roads. The laws against mendicancy in all countries were suspended in favour of scholars wandering in pursuit of knowledge, and formal licenses were

issued to them to ask alms. At home, at his college, the scholar's fare was the hardest, his lodging the barest. If rich in mind, he was expected to be poor in body; and so deeply was this theory grafted into English feeling that earls and dukes, when they began to frequent universities, shared the common simplicity. The furniture of a noble earl's room at an English university at present may cost, including the pictures of opera-dancers and race-horses and such like, perhaps five hundred pounds. When the magnificent Earl of Essex was sent to Cambridge, in Elizabeth's time, his guardians provided him with a deal table covered in green baize, a truckle bed, half-a-dozen chairs, and a wash-hand basin. The cost of all, I think, was five pounds.[6]

Froude later adds:

The scholar was held in high honour, but his contribution to the commonwealth was not appreciable in money, and was not rewarded with money. He went without what he could not produce, that he might keep his independence and his self-respect unharmed. Neither scholarship nor science starved under this treatment; more noble souls have been smothered in luxury than were ever killed by hunger.

That, says Froude, 'was the old English education which formed the character of the English and Scotch nations'. The apprenticeship system is dying away 'as no longer suited to what is called modern civilization'. The discipline of poverty, he regrets, has gone in England although not at that time totally in Scotland. We have got instead, said Froude, 'what we called enlarged minds'. And he did not want the young men of his audience to be bewitched by the notion of the enlarged mind. The world was changing, for sure, and they should adapt to it, but not by giving up the old principles. A man could do his job but without losing what was essential in the old order: honesty, absence of greed and doing the job well rather than always thinking about 'pushing ahead'. In the Middle Ages the trades and professions created their own wealth and the scholars didn't need it, or at least not very much. That surely is a lesson for today when education absorbs such large amounts of taxpayers' money. The lessons for today will be considered at the end of this chapter and I do not doubt that is the light in which Froude himself, if he were here, would want his work to be applied. No doubt he would think that much of our own modern education has as its aim what his friend John Ruskin called the confidence to 'knock at the double-belled door' or its modern equivalent.

Froude goes on to condemn the demands of education in his day as quite ridiculous. It means, he says, 'instruction in everything which human beings have done, thought or discovered; all history, all languages, all sciences'. He gives an example:

> When the competitive examination system was first set on foot, a board of examiners met to draw up their papers of questions. The scale of requirement had first to be settled. Among them a highly distinguished man, who was to examine in English history, announced that, for himself, he meant to set a paper for which Macaulay might possibly get full marks; and he wished the rest of the examiners to imitate him in the other subjects. I saw the paper which he set. I could myself have answered two questions out of a dozen. And it was gravely expected that ordinary young men of twenty-one, who were to be examined also in Greek and Latin, in moral philosophy, in ancient history, in mathematics, and in two modern languages, were to show a proficiency in each and all of these subjects, which a man of mature age and extraordinary talents, like Macaulay, who had devoted his whole time to that special study, had attained only in one of them.[7]

Froude, of course, pointed out that the old universities were struggling against these absurdities. The only difference between the student of those days and the old scholar is that he learns no lessons of poverty: 'in his three years' course he will have tasted luxuries unknown to him at home'. And, he adds: 'An Oxford education fits a man extremely well for the trade of gentleman'.

In his own time, Froude recognises, it was becoming necessary to alter all this. He points out that everyone was agreed about the Three R's which were followed by Latin and Greek because the universities demanded them. Then followed "textbooks", "abridgements", "elements" or 'whatever they are called' to keep up with the kind of knowledge that the 1851 Exhibition necessitated. And all this at that time for satisfying examiners. To return to his own words: 'To cram a lad's mind with the names of things he never handled, places he never saw or will see, statements of facts which he cannot possibly understand, and must remain merely words to him – this, in my opinion, is like loading his stomach with marbles'.[8] At the heart of Froude's concept of education is the simple idea of uniting facts with experience and, of course, he was just as critical of history being understood purely in terms of facts which had long since ceased to be meaningfully verifiable. In education clearly he wanted a boy to learn facts for which he would see the use. He then turns to one of those contrasts he loved to use to drive home his point. 'Lord Brougham,' he tells us, 'once said that he hoped the time would come when every man in England would read Bacon. William Cobbett, that you may have heard of, said that he would be contented when every man in England would eat bacon'.[9]

How much of the failure of the Victorian education system still remains with us and what parts of ours are the logical outcome of what was happening then? The sort of sharp lad without the restraints of the fundamental moral training that Froude spoke of so approvingly, might well make a name for himself in today's media, or in advertising or even in the most respectable professions and cause them to be brought into disrepute in the eyes of the general public. Probably the way in which the enormous quantities of information, far greater than in Froude's day, have been accommodated, is by more and more specialisation. One of the wisest remarks on the subject came from Froude's contemporary Thomas Huxley who proposed that in Higher Education the student should aim at 'knowing everything about something and something about everything'. Thereby he would know something in depth and have an idea about how other subjects might relate to his own, i.e. understand in principle the meaning of depth. Unfortunately, we seem to be moving towards experts who, as is commonly admitted, seem to be learning more and more about less and less and who fail to understand the part that their own knowledge plays in the whole unified pattern of experience.

Froude was ever ready to attack the economists of his day:

A great political economist has defended the existence of a luxuriously-living idle class as supplying a motive for exertion to those who are less highly favoured. They are like Olympian gods, condescending to their worshippers, 'Make money, money enough, and you and your descendants shall become as we are, and shoot grouse and drink champagne all the days of your lives'.

No doubt this would be a highly influential incitement to activity of a sort; only it must be remembered that there are many sorts of activity, and short smooth cuts to wealth as well as long hilly roads. In civilized and artificial communities there are many ways, where fools have money and rogues want it, of effecting a change of possession. The process is at once an intellectual pleasure, extremely rapid, and every way more agreeable than dull mechanical labour. I doubt very much indeed whether the honesty of the country has been improved by the substitution so generally of mental education for industrial; and the three R's, if no industrial training has gone along with them, are apt, as Miss Nightingale observes, to produce a fourth R of rascaldom.

Again morality, practical everyday honesty, is at the root of Froude's notion of education:

I accept without qualification the first principle of our forefathers, that every boy born into the world should be put in the way of maintaining himself in honest independence. No education which does not make this its first aim is worth anything at all. There are but three ways of living, as some one has said; by working, by begging, or by stealing. Those who do no work, disguise it in whatever pretty language we please, are doing one of the other two. A poor man's child is brought up here with no will of his own. We have no right to condemn him to be a mendicant or rogue; he may fairly demand therefore to be put in the way of earning his bread by labour. The practical necessities must take precedence of the intellectual. A tree must be rooted in the soil before it can bear flowers and fruit. A man must learn to stand upright upon his own feet, to respect himself, to be independent of charity or accident. It is on this basis only that any superstructure of intellectual cultivation worth having can possibly be built. The old apprentice-ship therefore was, in my opinion, an excellent system, as the world used to be. The Ten Commandments and a handicraft made a good and wholesome equipment to commence life with. Times are changed. The apprentice plan broke down: partly because it was abused for purposes of tyranny; partly because employers did not care to be burdened with boys whose labour was unprofitable; partly because it opened no road for exceptional clever lads to rise into higher positions; they were started in a groove from which they could never afterwards escape.[10]

In his day Froude was able to say that the original imperatives of the 'old Education' remain unchanged. No doubt fundamentally they remain unchanged today but the trends which were beginning in the Victorian era have developed and even a pretence of morality is vanishing, indeed is looked upon as a kind of hypocrisy. Anyone who looks at the television programme 'University Challenge' or listens to 'Brain of Britain' on the radio can hardly fail to come to the conclusion that even the remotest facts impress not merely a limited number of examiners in their ivory towers but the whole, or almost the whole, of today's so-called educated society. The speedy resort to lies is thought of as a perfectly understandable necessity of party politics, and in the personal sphere it is said to be an intrusion into privacy if a question is asked about the private lives of public figures. Froude, I am sure, would have required not only that they should appear to be above suspicion, but that they actually were so.

With the right foundation Froude was convinced that meaningful learning could be built upon it but even then he further stresses: 'Add knowledge afterwards, as much as you will, but let it be knowledge that will lead to doing better each particular work a boy is practicing.'[11] Froude was convinced that 'every occupation – I don't say the scavenger's or the chimney sweep's – but every productive occupation which adds something to the capital of mankind, if followed assiduously with a desire to understand everything connected with it, is an ascending stair whose summit is nowhere, and from the successive steps of which the horizon of knowledge perpetually enlarges.'

Froude gives examples and, not surprisingly, his initial one is the peasants in the field. Today perhaps we may know too much not too little about what can be done in our fields, without really understanding the possible long-term side effects. The story is plainly told in Richard Body's *Agriculture:*

The Triumph and the Shame. Froude must have understood that he was on dangerous ground – in both the literal and metaphorical senses – because he himself had been long railing against the Enclosure Acts which caused the peasant to lose his cottage and the chance of work around his own village or hamlet. He railed against the way the big farms were devouring small ones, making it necessary for the poor peasant to walk for about three hours in the morning to work and the same in the evening home. Here at St Andrew's he remarked: 'It may sound like mockery to talk thus of possible prospects of the toil-worn drudge who drags his limbs at the day's end to his straw pallet, sleeps heavily, and wakes only to renew the weary round. I am but comparing two systems of education'.[12]

It would make excellent sense to look at that comparison again today. With mass production and the even greater application of science, particularly electronic science, in almost every field of production, it is necessary to look again fundamentally at our system of education and production. The smart manager is finding that the easier way of improving immediate profits is to sack a large proportion of his workforce and bring in machinery, but in so doing he may in the longer term be reducing the 'customer base' for his goods. His machines certainly won't be buying them. Perhaps the area where we clearly have gone too far is in agribusiness. The peasant in the field has almost disappeared. There may be a good case for a more labour intensive approach. To achieve better quality food may need more small-scale agriculture and this in itself would require a more scientifically equipped peasant or at least more intelligent supervision of the so-called humble peasant. Were he alive today, I believe Froude would have condemned with no less rigour our faults than he did the faults of his day. The headlong rush into what appear to be scientific solutions certainly characterise both ages, and both have had the attraction of easy money, easy wealth.

There was a strong practical element in Froude, whose family generations back had been yeoman farmers in Devon, and who had once even thought seriously of going out to Australia to make his living in sheep or cattle. His attitude was sometimes reminiscent of Emerson's, whose down-to-earth thinking so deeply influenced the course of American history down to the present day.

Froude moves on to the professions: doctors, lawyers, engineers, ministers of religion: 'Bodies become deranged, affairs become deranged, sick souls require their sores to be attended to'.[13] In these professions, there is still an element of apprenticeship, even today. Here, however, Froude considers the role of the university: 'I am well aware that a professional education cannot be completed at a university: but it is true also that with every profession there is a theoretic or scientific groundwork which can be learned nowhere so well, and, if these precious years are wasted on what is useless, will never be learned properly at all'.

In this regard the twentieth century took note, I believe, of what Froude had been saying but overlooked his moral strictures not only to the workers and their unions but also to those with higher responsibilities. I think he would have agreed with the old Naval saying, 'When there's trouble on the lower deck, sack the Captain'. Froude was the enemy of all false high-mindedness: 'The principle which I advocate is of the earth, earthy. We are ourselves made of earth; our work is on the earth; and most of us are commonplace people, who are obliged to make the most of our time. History, poetry, logic, moral philosophy, classical literature are excellent as ornament. We had a theory at Oxford that our system, however defective in many ways, yet developed in us some especially precious human qualities.'[14]

This is at the heart of what Froude took issue with in his time. It was especially supposed to produce clergymen. He expected that if it really did so the effect should have been considerable and yet 'from the great houses in the city to the village grocer, the commercial life of England has been saturated with fraud. So deep has it been that a strictly honest tradesman can hardly hold his own against the competition'. And yet, as Froude famously complained, the Church was worried about the colour of ecclesiastical petticoats. Froude cried out in his time for a little common honesty, which might not be too bad an idea today!

During the previous thirty years he had heard many sermons but never one that he could recollect on the 'primitive Commandments': thou shalt not lie, thou shalt not steal. Since his time we have had the Weights and Measures Act and at that level a little more honesty may be found, but at a higher level, if a fraction of what is related in the newspapers is to be believed, the situation has got no better, but probably worse.

The biggest change since those Victorian days has been the introduction of mass production and electronic controls and communication. This has enabled the international corporation to develop, sometimes with the morals of the worst village grocer. What is plainly evident, however, is that the moral imperative, in deed as well as word, which Froude, Ruskin and Carlyle stressed as the first principle of education is equally lacking today and equally necessary. The principle Froude wanted to take from our ancestors of the Middle Ages applied to poor scholars might also be applied to a wide range of modern studies – media studies in particular where success and monetary reward often seems to depend on dishonesty. Froude has some especially interesting views on the literature of his day:

> Literature happens to be the only occupation in which wages are not in proportion to the goodness of the work done. It is not that they are generally small, but the adjustment of them is awry. It is true that in all callings nothing great will be produced if the first object be what you can make by them. To do what you do well should be the first thing, the wages the second; but except in the instances of which I am speaking, the rewards of a man are in proportion to his skill and industry. The best carpenter receives the highest pay. The better he works, the better for his prospects. The best lawyer, the best doctor, commands most practice and makes the largest fortune. But with literature, a different element is introduced into the problem. The present rule on which authors are paid is by the page and the sheet; the more words the more pay. It ought to be exactly the reverse. Great poetry, great philosophy, great scientific discovery, every intellectual production which has genius, work, and permanence in it, is the fruit of long thought and patient and painful elaboration. Work of this kind, done hastily, would be better not done at all. When completed, it will be small in bulk; it will address itself for a long time to the few and not

to the many. The reward for it will not be measurable, and not obtainable in money except after many generations, when the brain out of which it was spun has long returned to its dust. Only by accident is a work of genius immediately popular, in the sense of being widely bought.[15]

Some interesting examples follow and an injunction that if any of his hearers want to make money they should follow a trade in which it is legitimate to do so. This did not mean that Froude denied higher or spiritual values. Earlier in the address he made the point with unmistakable emphasis: High above all occupations which have their beginning and end in the seventy years of mortal life, stand undoubtedly the unproductive callings which belong to the spiritual culture.[16]

The address covers a few more of Froude's favourite themes, including Empire and emigration, for which he apologises.

What I insist upon is, generally, that in a country like ours, where each child that is born among us finds every acre of land appropri-ated, a universal 'Not yours' set upon the rich things with which he is surrounded, and a government which, unlike those of old Greece or modern China, does not permit superfluous babies to be strangled - such a child, I say, since he is required to live, has a right to demand such teaching as shall enable him to live with honesty, and take such a place in society as belongs to the faculties which he has brought with him. It is a right which was recognized in one shape or another by our ancestors. It must be recognized now and always, if we are not to become a mutinous rabble. And it ought to be the guiding principle of all education, high and low. We have not to look any longer to this island only. There is an abiding place now for Englishmen and Scots wherever our flag is flying. This narrow Britain, once our only home, has become the breeding place and nursery of a race which is spreading over the world. Year after year we are swarming as the bees swarm; and year after year, and I hope more and more, high-minded young men of all ranks will prefer free air and free elbow-room for mind and body to the stool and desk of the dingy office, the ill paid drudgery of the crowded ranks of the professions, or the hopeless labour of our home farmsteads and workshops.

Education always should contemplate this larger sphere, and cultivate the capacities which will command success there. Britain may have yet a future before it grander than its past; instead of a country standing alone, complete in itself, it may become the metropolis of an enormous and coherent empire: but on this condition only, that her children, when they leave her shores, shall look back upon her, not – like the poor Irish when they fly to America – as a stepmother who gave them stones for bread, but as a mother to whose care and nurture they shall owe their after prosperity. Whether this shall be so, whether England has reached its highest point of greatness, and will now descend to a second place among the nations, or whether it has yet before it another era of brighter glory, depends on ourselves, and depends more than anything on the breeding which we give to our children. The boy that is kindly natured, and wisely taught and assisted to make his way in life, does not forget his father and his mother. He is proud of his family, and jealous for the honour of the name he bears. If the million lads that swarm in our towns and villages are so trained that at home or in the colonies they can provide for themselves, without passing first through a painful interval of suffering, they will be loyal wherever they may be; good citizens at home, and still Englishmen and Scotsmen on the Canadian lakes or in New Zealand. Our island shores will be stretched till they cover half the globe. It was not so that we colonized America, and we are reaping now the reward of our carelessness. We sent America our convicts. We sent America our Pilgrim Fathers, flinging them out as worse than felons. We said to the Irish cottier, You are a burden upon the rates; go find a home elsewhere. Had we offered him a home in the enormous territories that belong to us, we might have sent him to places where he would have been no burden but a blessing. But we bade him carelessly go where he would, and shift as he could for himself; he went with a sense of burning wrong, and he left a festering sore behind him. Injustice and heedlessness have borne their proper fruits. We have raised up against us a mighty empire to be the rival, it may be the successful rival, of our power.

Loyalty, love of kindred, love of country, we know not what we are doing when we trifle with feelings the most precious and beautiful that belong to us – most beautiful, most enduring, most hard to be obliterated – yet feelings which, when they are obliterated, cannot change to neutrality and cold friendship. Americans still, in spite of themselves, speak of England as home. They tell us they must be our brothers or our enemies, and which of the two they will ultimately be is still uncertain.[17]

He closes with a warning to young men, which surely must be true in every age. The details differ but the temptations remain the same at all times:

> We live in times of change – political change, intellectual change, change of all kinds. You whose minds are active, especially such of you as give yourselves much to speculation, will be drawn inevitably into profoundly interesting and perplexing questions, of which our fathers and grandfathers knew nothing. Practical men engaged in business take formulas for granted. They cannot be forever running to first principles. They hate to see established opinions disturbed. Opinions, however, will and must be disturbed from time to time. There is no help for it. The minds of ardent and clever students are particularly apt to move fast in these directions; and thus when they go out in the world, they find themselves exposed to one of two temptations, according to their temperament: either to lend themselves to what is popular and plausible, to conceal their real convictions, to take up with what we call in England humbug, to humbug others, or, perhaps, to keep matters smoother, to humbug themselves; or else to quarrel violently with things which they imagine to be passing away, and which they consider should be quick in doing it, as having no basis in truth. A young man of ability now-a-days is extremely likely to be tempted into one or other of these lines. The first is the more common on my side of the Tweed; the harsher and more thorough-going, perhaps, on yours. Things are changing, and have to change, but they change very slowly. The established authorities are in possession of the field, and are naturally desirous to keep it. And there is no kind of service which they more eagerly reward than the support of clever fellows who have dipped over the edge of latitudinarianism, who profess to have sounded the disturbing currents of the intellectual seas, and discovered that they are accidental or unimportant.
>
> On the other hand, men who cannot get away with this kind of thing are likely to be exasperated into unwise demonstrativeness, to become radicals in politics and radicals in thought. Their private disapprobation bursts into open enmity; and this road too, if they continue long upon it, leads to unhealthy conclusions. No one can thrive upon denials: positive truth of some kind is essential as food both for mind and character. Depend upon it that in all long-established practices or spiritual formulas there has been some

living truth; and if you have not discovered and learnt to respect it, you do not yet understand the questions which you are in a hurry to solve. And again, intellectually impatient people should remember the rules of social courtesy, which forbid us in private to say things, however true, which can give pains to others. These rules, if they do not absolutely forbid us to obtrude opinions which offend those who do not share them, yet require us to pause and consider. Our thoughts and our conduct are our own. We may say justly to any one, You shall not make me profess to think true what I believe to be false; you shall not make me do what I do not think just: but there our natural liberty ends. Others have as good a right to their opinion as we have to ours. To any one who holds what are called advanced views on serious subjects, I recommend a long suffering reticence and the reflection that, after all, he may possibly be wrong. Whether we are Radicals or Conservatives we require to be often reminded that truth or falsehood, justice or injustice, are no creatures of our own belief. We cannot make true feelings false, or false feelings true, by choosing to think them so. We cannot vote right into wrong or wrong into right. The eternal truths and rights of things exist, fortunately, independent of our thoughts or wishes, fixed as mathematics, inherent in the nature of man and the world. They are no more to be trifled with than gravitation. If we discover and obey them, it is well with us; but that is all we can do.[18]

And a final note:

Of all the evil spirits abroad at this hour in the world, *insincerity* is the most dangerous.[19]

In our modern world the complaint may be heard that Froude is always referring to men and boys. He certainly was but he was speaking to an audience of young men. Men were following the false dreams of 'bettering themselves,' 'raising their position in the world' and the like. Froude, I am sure, would have guessed that if men set up these idols and women backed them in their ambitions, it would not be long before women wanted to go after them for themselves. A little anecdote illustrates the balance of his concern. In a letter to a friend he wrote: 'Ten days ago my second daughter was happily brought into the world, with singularly little suffering for anybody. We hope it will be a symbol of the life which is to be.

People condole me on the sex, and I rather consider myself to be congratulated.'[20]

There is not much doubt that Froude was in many ways ahead of his times and therefore well worth reading today, especially his address on education – not as a way of peering into a corner of the nineteenth century but for what he offers to a progressively complicating twenty-first century.

Chapter 3
Religion

Heaven from all creatures hides the book of fate,
All but the page prescribed, their present state.

Alexander Pope

In 1871,[1] Froude began his lecture at St Andrews on Calvinism and indeed on all the other branches of religion in the Western world: 'Religious men, it is sometimes said, express themselves in all moods and all tenses except the present indicative.' And went on a little later to say, 'systems of religion have been vigorous and effective precisely to the extent which they have seen in the existing order of things the hand of a living ruler'. I originally intended to take almost the whole of Froude's lecture and make it the chapter on religion. I thought it a unique overall survey of the subject and far better than anything I could manage to produce. However, wise friends convinced me that it unbalanced the book. I reluctantly agreed simply to pick out some of the highlights and relate them to the 'Froude Today' theme but not without agreeing that I should put the lecture in full in an appendix and strongly advise the reader to regard it as integral to the text. I have added two other important pieces: the Short Study on Luther and Erasmus, and the other on the Prospects for

Protestantism, which includes an analysis of an evangelical meeting. It is interesting to note how nations at the height of their power tend to have strong religious movements and to compare the situation in America today with Froude's description of what was happening at the height of the British Empire.

Froude had been through his baptism of fire at Oxford. In 1848 he published his *Nemesis of Faith*, a novel questioning some of the foundations of the religion of his day. He had been ordained and was a fellow of Oriel College. The book was regarded as so dangerous that it was publicly burnt and he was expelled from Oxford, not to return until Lord Salisbury asked him to become Regius Professor of Modern History for the last two years of his life.

In introducing that lecture to today's world it is perhaps best to start with its ending rather than its beginning: 'What the thing is which we call ourselves we know not. It may be true – I for one care not if it be – that the descent of our mortal bodies may be traced through an ascending series to some glutinous organism on the rocks of the primeval ocean. It is nothing to me how the Maker of me has been pleased to construct the perishable frame I call my body. It is *mine* but it is not *me*. The, intellectual spirit, being an·οὐσία – an essence – we believe it to be an incorruptible something from another source.' St Paul speaks of the same thing when he says 'I yet not I,' and refers to the dichotomy of the spiritual and the natural man. The Victorian argument ran that you could not reconcile man, the creature descended from apes, with man made in the image of God. We hear that argument again today in some of the states of the USA. Disraeli, at the Bishops' Conference at Oxford, famously and with his characteristic light touch, said that he was on the side of the angels. Froude's description of the occasion in his biography of Disraeli is well worth reading.

What is abundantly clear from his lecture is that Froude was anxious to peel away all the falsehood that had become attached to religion. He was as hard on the Protestants of his own day as he was on the Catholics of the 16th century, attacking the idolatry of the latter and what he called the bibliolatry of the other, saying that the Evangelicals used the words of Luther and Calvin without giving them the meaning that the original Protestants put into them; and he was no less scathing of other faiths which had degenerated from their original intention. A superficial literalism is still today characteristic of many evangelical groups, especially in the United States. Paradoxically it probably has its source in the literalistic tendency of the scientific method. In their sermons and writings Luther and Calvin, Bunyan and Knox exhibit nothing of this kind of limitation but dig deeply into the meaning and interpretation of the actual words of the scriptures.

Carefully avoiding technical theology, Froude set out to show that we have to reconcile ourselves with the stringent forms of Calvinism which he believes were necessary in hard ages to combat fierce tyranny. Luther was an altogether different and sunnier character than Calvin who seldom laughed, but then he could afford to be so since he had the protection of his sovereign against the sword and the fires of his enemies. Froude clearly does not relish the severity of Calvin but feels that he must be judged in the light of the conditions in which he had to struggle.[1]

In the argument between predestination and free will Froude veers towards predestination. 'Free will commends itself to our feelings.' 'Calvinism is nearer to the facts however harsh and forbidding those facts may seem'.[2] The latest scientific developments seem to veer more or less in the same direction. There appear to be two sets of determinants: the inner and the outer. The inner are viewed in terms of genetic makeup. The outer are the environment and this even includes the environment within the womb, which may have a very powerful effect on the creation of character. Certainly there is an interaction between the two. Froude put it this way: 'The moral system of the universe is like a document written in alternate ciphers which change from line to line. We read a sentence but at the next our key fails us'.[3] The point has been made recently by genetic scientists that determinism is not the same thing as inevitability, particularly in cases where two sets of determinants conflict. It seems that Christianity preaches, emphatically so in Froude's view, obedience to the inner determinants. Christ said the

Kingdom of Heaven is within you, and the Book of Common Prayer speaks of a god 'whose service is perfect freedom' (service in this context should be bond-service). If there is a moral system, albeit written in alternate ciphers, then the paradox appears to be explained. Freedom is doing what your inner nature demands. The Calvinists called this inner eye the Inspiration of the Almighty and Froude certainly saw the strength of this belief as the power enabling them to face the vicissitudes and villainies of the outer world. As Froude puts it, 'when emotion and sentiment and tender imaginative piety have become the handmaids of superstition, and have dreamt themselves into forgetfulness that there is any difference between lies and truth – the slavish form of belief called Calvinism, in one or other of its many forms, has borne ever an inflexible front to illusion and mendacity, and has preferred to be ground to powder like flint than to bend before violence, or melt under enervating temptation.'[4]

What is even more significant is the way in which Froude sees different degrees of insight in different people and varying levels of collective insight in the different faiths of the Western world. 'There seems, in the first place,' he writes, 'to lie in all men, in proportion to their understanding, a conviction that there is in all human things a real order and purpose, notwithstanding the chaos in which at times they seem to be involved.'

Froude starts with what the Greeks meant by the Ἀνάγκη or destiny which he says is at rock bottom moral Providence. Job and Prometheus proclaim the same message. He later goes on to the Egyptians who had a highly complex religious system with stern religious duties notwithstanding the injustice at the base of it. The corruption of it and of its priests was highlighted by Ahknaton, who for a few short years attempted to establish a monotheistic faith based on the idea of 'living with Truth'. Although his efforts failed in Egypt they played their part in inspiring the Israelites to escape their servitude and face the tribulations of the wilderness with hope one day of entering the Promised Land. What they found there was 'an idolatry yet fouler and more cruel than what they had left behind them.' They trampled it out, Froude tells us, by military means and he says: 'They were not perfect – very far from perfect. An army at best is made up of mixed materials, and war, of all ways of making wrong into right, is the harshest; but they were directed by a noble purpose, and they have left a mark never to be effaced in the history of the human race.' Like all good causes, Froude sees that of the Israelites over hundreds of years degenerating into rituals and superstitions notwithstanding the warnings of their prophets. Froude mentions Tacitus and the stoics before coming on to the contrast between their individual discipline and the message of the Galilean fishermen and the tent-maker of Tarsus to the toiling millions.

Having already considered the sturdy mountain tribes of Persia who spread the teachings of Zoroaster, whose strength eventually gave way to luxury and corruption as seems to occur with all noble causes in this world, Froude goes on to consider Islam and with it perhaps comes a ray of special light on today's dilemma with the threat of terror and savagery, not less terrible than anything that the ancient world could exhibit. He regarded Islam as inferior to Christianity: 'The light there was in it was but reflected from the sacred books of the Jews and Arab traditions.' It taught something real: the omnipotence and omnipresence of the one eternal Spirit. It left very little room for heresy and argument. Froude knew that in his day the Koran was criticised for countenancing sensual vice, but he retorted 'it bridled and brought within limits a sensuality which before was unbounded.' On the one hand he argued the superiority of Christianity by comparing the example of the Apostle Paul with no weapon but his word and by himself submitting to be killed, to the fierce Kaled calling himself the sword of the Almighty. Nevertheless the Koran forbade and absolutely extinguished, wherever Islam is professed, the bestial drunkenness which is the disgrace of our English and Scottish towns. 'Even now,' he emphasises, 'the Mussulman probably governs his life by the Koran more accurately than most Christians obey the Sermon on the Mount or the Ten Commandments.'⁵ In this context it might just be appropriate to quote a piece by Richard Ingrams in an article he wrote for The Observer in mid-2004:

Quite apart from any acts of terrorism, the so-called preacher of hate, Abu Hamza, now facing extradition to the United States, is also accused in the media of having consistently mocked and derided our British values.

This is a somewhat vaguer offence than anything to do with the Taliban or al-Qaeda. But as these so-called values are also on the lips of Mr Blair and co these days, it might be helpful to try to define what exactly is involved.

The cleric, let it be said, has been a bit more specific and outspoken on the question than the Prime Minister. Speaking of our once great nation he says: 'They want only to look at nude pictures, go to football matches, have a few pints and go to sleep. They have become slaves.'

That is not the sort of thing that anyone like Mr Blair would ever say, though it is perfectly acceptable verdict from someone like Mr Hamza, who is described as a religious leader.

In the past – 40 or 50 years ago, perhaps – one could imagine the Archbishop of Canterbury expressing the same sort of concerns as Abu Hamza, though he might have put it rather differently, expressing what he would have called 'disquiet over the growing materialism of modern society ... the increasingly pornographic nature of some of our newspapers ... the worrying increase in alcoholism ... all tending to undermine that spirit of enterprise and initiative that once made the country great'.

No archbishop would nowadays dare to voice such concerns (they are more likely to preach against global warming or speed cameras). It has been left to the mad mullah of Finsbury Park to speak out. But now even his voice has been silenced.[6]

The message is clear. Unless we view the world situation from the perspective of a moral system such as Froude describes we are not likely to escape a catastrophic clash which will dwarf the old conflict of the Cold War. Froude continued with a brief description of the gigantic system of supernationalism by which the Roman Catholic Church of the later Middle Ages spread its power over the whole of Western Europe. The Reformation, in Froude's view, was as entirely justified as was the revolt of the Israelites from their captivity in Egypt. Nevertheless he could speak well of the Roman Catholic priests in Ireland when, in his view, they promoted a simple and practical morality among the peasants, and condemn the falsehood in his own country of charging the Catholic priests with preaching Fenian sermons from their pulpits. This was interesting indeed from a man only too ready to condemn the decadence of religions and priests wherever he detected the hypocrisy of it.

At rock bottom Froude believed there were two religions: the religion of nature which developed heathen practices of worshipping animals as well as inhuman rituals and idolatry in the widest sense, on the one hand, and on the other, spiritual religion based on a moral system that would be known by its fruits not its words. The latter would always be subject to degeneration and men and priests would find loopholes to avoid its stern commandments, and this in its turn lead to social injustice. Froude saw individual morality and social justice as inextricably linked. He certainly saw a code involving a few personal moral rules but leaving people free to do what they liked at the wider social level as entirely unsatisfactory, and he railed incessantly against the prevailing political economic theories. If the individual did what was right it would produce a just society but he was not convinced that egalitarian distribution could simply be superimposed. The laws governing human behaviour were essentially just as clear-cut as those applying to the simplest example in physics. Christianity properly understood had a truly gentle side which most other religions did not have. Its message of forgiveness was not one which said you can confess and go on to do the same again. It said you must root out the wish to sin. Christ did not condemn the woman taken in adultery but neither did he say go away and do it again. He knew that not condemning her would change her heart and her wish, He said go and sin no more. He upheld the Law and the prophets to their inmost meaning. This was why Luther said if you sin, sin boldly. Blake similarly, while emphasising Christian forgiveness, warned of the danger of the festering suppressed desires. The New Testament does not demand less than the Old. It demands more. Jesus Christ said not only that good acts were necessary but that they had to proceed from a pure heart. Only the pure in heart were blessed and only they would see the Kingdom of Heaven. So desperate is our human condition that only after a process like that which Bunyan's Pilgrim went through, or like that which William James describes in the chapter on the Sick Soul in his *Varieties of Religious Experience*, can true Christian forgiveness be experienced. Dunn's biography clearly shows that Froude had been though something like that and it distinguishes both him and John Ruskin from the light-hearted salvationists of their day. It also explains why Froude said that they used the words that Luther and Calvin used but didn't mean what they meant. Christian forgiveness is about forgiving ourselves, not about churches or priests forgiving us. Luther made this very clear. In his writings the Devil is the Accuser.

Despite all this, and this is the paradox at the heart of Luther's thinking, he like Froude, and indeed like the prophets of Israel, proclaimed a moral universe. The laws of the universe were absolute, Froude tells us, adding: 'No Pope can dispense with a statute enrolled in the Chancery of Heaven, or popular vote repeal it'.[7] Popes tend not to attempt it today but popular votes are often expected to make black white and white black

In all of Froude's writings on religion there is one single thread running through them. There must be the fruits of a right position. No self-righteousness, no hypocrisy. It is clear that he thought that all faiths insofar as they are endeavouring to separate truth from falsehood, right from wrong in a simple down to earth way, have a common thread running through them. Our Western culture has underlying it the Christian ethic and that is rooted in the literature of the Jews and the Arabs. Recognising that is of paramount importance today and those who speak of 'people of the Book' are in fact seeking an understanding between Christians, Jews and Muslims which is the only path to avoid global disaster. A shallow cosmopolitan secularism will never be enough to curb the arrogance of the human will, of which the twentieth century gave us but a taste of what could be,

At the very heart of religious thinking that deserves the name is the notion that things are not as they seem. Froude says it in this way: '... and without an illogical but nonetheless a positive certainty that things are not as they seem – that in spite of appearance, there is justice at the heart of them, and that, in the working out of the vast drama, justice will assert somehow and somewhere its sovereign right and power, the better sort of person would find existence unendurable.'[8] The Platonic aspect of Froude's thinking is apparent in this crucial but not emphasised passage. It is immediately evident that almost all he says hinges on this one concept. Indeed that the whole of Western Culture has grown out of that way of understanding which Plato expressed in his allegory of the cave in the *Republic*. Today it is reflected in the words of the Prince of Wales: 'It seems to be becoming harder and harder in this age to stick to what we believe – or feel. We are told constantly that we have to live in the 'real world' – but the 'real world' is within us. The reality is that 'Truth, Goodness and Beauty' in the outer, manifested world are only made possible through the inner invisible pattern – the unmanifested archetype.'[9]

Great as were the works of Aristotle in influencing the development of the physical sciences, the overall influence of the School of Athens has been in the direction in which Plato pointed. Where it has not prevailed materialism, the arrogance of man and often barbarism of the most objectionable and almost inconceivable kind has been the consequence. Sadly Marxism wherever it has spread has had the effect of throwing out the baby of insight with the bath water of superstition. Wherever Platonic thinking, in contrast, has spread it has had the effect of raising the level of civilization. Two examples must suffice to demonstrate it. Augustus in founding the Roman Empire consciously based his thinking on the writings of Plato, and whatever terrible things may have happened to it later, it was Gibbon who told us that it probably provided the best period for the majority of mankind up to his own times.

Christianity reinforced by the Platonist thinking of St. Augustine of Hippo, after the Dark Ages, brought forth Medieval civilization from which Froude believed we had much to learn and whose small city states (created on St Augustine's recommendation) were so beloved by Leopold Kohr, author of the book, *The Breakdown of Nations*.

Chapter 4

The Acceptable Faces of Capitalism and Communism

The evil sisters: poverty and luxury.
James Anthony Froude

After his depressing experience at Oxford Froude took a job as a tutor to the son of Samuel Darbyshire, a highly successful solicitor in Manchester. It was here that he not only had the opportunity to meet many of his employer's famous friends, including Elizabeth Gaskell and Charles Hallé, but also to come into close contact with the 'real' and tough worlds of business and commerce. Darbyshire was very kind to him and, had he wished it Dunn tells us, would have found him a position in his own firm of solicitors, but Froude had made up his mind that come what may he would face the harsh world of literature, but not until he had become acquainted with some of Manchester's practical businessmen. The contrast between Oxford and Manchester must have made a deep impression on his mind. It is easy to see how this must have influenced what he said to the students at St Andrews much later in his life. In his own biographical notes he described how he had been influenced for a time by the writings of George Sand and Louis Blanc. Communism, at a time when the equal distribution of wealth was in the air in Paris, developed not merely in France but also spread to many young minds in the rest of Europe as well as America. Froude described how reality struck him:

> I was speaking one day with a manufacturer, an advanced radical in Politics and not disinclined to listen to any reasonable proposals about a fairer division of the profits of business between the capitalist and the workman. A notion lies at the bottom of much of the dissatisfaction that, if all were treated fairly, each man would be as well off as he sees his employers to be. 'Be sure of your facts,' said my friend. 'I employ a thousand hands. I pay them each on an average a pound a week, or in a year £52,000. The entire returns of my business are about £70,000. Of this, £10,000 goes to the capital account; £3,000 to other necessary outgoings; £5,000 remains to me and my family, in return for which I have all the risk, all the trouble of management, all the loss in bad times. Distribute my £5,000 and turn the £52,000 into £57,000: pass it over with all the trouble and all the uncertainty, and how much will each of my men have gained by the transaction?
>
> I never worried about Communism again from that moment.'[1]

Froude follows this with his own description of how he was affected by Manchester: 'It cured me for ever,' he wrote, 'of the unwholesome speculative habits which grew up so easily in university life', a view that brought him closer to Emerson in America. After that spell in Manchester he was more certain than ever that he wanted to rescue his 'clouded reputation' and devote himself to literature.

Froude's fundamental rejection, root and branch, of the communist way of thinking did not preclude him from making the most savage attacks on corruption of all kinds in the business world, or indeed in the political sphere as already shown in the chapter on education. He denounced the dishonesty of his age as roundly as any man or woman of Victorian times, not excluding Carlyle and Ruskin, but nonetheless heartily disliked the idea of 'instant' revolution because he always believed that real and worthwhile changes take place over many generations. Thus it is not surprising that when he thought of some of his famous contemporaries at Oxford he wrote:

For myself I never believed in an English revolution. I could see no signs that the noisy shouts of a hungry multitude were likely to upset a system so strongly based as ours then was, nor could I believe that an armed insurrection, even if successful, would mend the condition of any human being.'[2]

Nevertheless, he always sympathised with the oppressed and wanted to see their condition mended. This led him to oppose much of liberal doctrine of his day. His case is graphically put in his biography of Disraeli, (also quoted in my original article of Froude):

Under the old organisation of England, the different orders of men were bound together under reciprocal obligations of duty. The economists and their political followers held that duty had nothing to do with it. Food, wages and all else had their market value, which could be interfered with only to the general injury. The employer was to hire his labourers or his hands at the lowest rate at which they could be induced to work. If he ceased to need them, or if they would not work on terms which could remunerate him, he was at liberty to turn them off. The labourers, in return, might make the best of their own opportunity, and sell their services to the best advantage which competition allowed. The capitalists found the arrangement satisfactory to them. The people found it less satisfactory, and they replied by Chartism and rick-burnings.[3]

Once again his emphasis is upon an order based on duty, not on economics and money. The kind of society that Froude would like to see established is actually brought about, not by hasty politicians but by the kind of clear thinking that sometimes develops and establishes itself over many generations. That he believed in listening to a wide variety of serious opinions is demonstrated by all accounts of his editorship of *Frazers Magazine* and the range of articles which it included, a fact that enabled Bret Hart, as has already been said, to describe him as a democrat in the true sense of the word. He was able to respond to people, however mistaken he might himself consider them, if he believed their 'secret motives and passions' were sincere and grounded in personal integrity. A very good example of this is to be found in his own comments on his correspondence with General Cluseret, the communist general in Paris:

> I should like to show ... what these agitations really do mean. The socialist epidemic is not peculiar to this country. It is seen in America, and all over Europe. The essential doctrines of it among the true believers are the same everywhere, although they are flavoured a little differently to suit national tastes. A good many persons here may have heard of General Cluseret. He is a very remarkable man. He was a French officer originally, but served with distinction in the Civil War of America. When it was over he was selected to head the then intended Irish-American insurrection of 1867. He was, I believe, the original of the 'General' whom Lord Beaconsfield describes with so much appreciation in *Lothair*. For a month or six weeks he commanded the Communist army in Paris in 1871. He had been deposed before the catastrophe on account of his moderation and good sense. If he could, he would have prevented the murder of the Archbishop of Paris, and he endangered his life in his attempt to do so. He escaped after Paris was taken, and as he was more feared than any of the Communist leaders he would have been instantly shot had he been caught. I have had much correspondence with him at various times. He is a practical, temperate, and exceedingly able man. He is now again living openly in Paris, and has just published his memoirs. For a volume and a half you read these memoirs with pleasure. You do not agree with his views, but they are not violently expressed, and you respect his honesty, capacity, and courage.[4]

Froude resisted all attempts to persuade him to join a political party. Politicians, he said, 'were like men who having been given two eyes by nature deliberately extinguished one'. Not surprisingly he was much happier editing *Frazers Magazine*. That gave him the opportunity to give expression to a range of opinions many of which were far removed from his own. For Froude political decisions were always a matter for very fine judgement and could not be settled by the cries of a crowd – which is what much of our modern mass voting system amounts to – and yet he always bore in mind what ordinary people in a settled mind would regard as fair and satisfactory. The Victorian Parliament he despised. Referring to the new industrial classes he wrote: 'These classes, powerful though they may be, and in Parliament a great deal too powerful, are not the people of England'.

An almost perfect example of how Froude dealt with an overexcited public and with the influences that excited them occurred in 1870. A second 'Crimean War' threatened. Dunn's excellent description of how Froude handled the situation highlights the practical side of Froude as well as his ability to intervene successfully in the course of political events:

Throughout 1870 the English press was busy with the demands which the Russians were making for release from treaty obligations which they considered unjust. Feeling ran high and threats of war filled the air. Froude was familiar with such clamour. He wanted no repetition of the unwisdom which had led to the Crimean War. He was for a cool, dispassionate study of conditions, and a course of action just and honourable to both sides. At a meeting in the Town Hall of Birmingham on 2nd December 1870, he supported the resolution 'That whilst this meeting disapproves of the manner in which the Russian Government has disclaimed certain obligations entered into under the Treaty of Paris, and condemns the abrogation of any treaty unless by the consent of the signatories thereto, it protests against an appeal to arms, considering that the subject in dispute ought to be referred to a European Congress.'

His remarks were warmly received and well reported. He urged that all threats of an ultimatum, all jingoistic clamour, should be put aside, and that the nations concerned should seriously consider whether or not Russia had just grievances. To this end, he defined the term 'treaty' and considered the nature of treaties in general, some of which, he pointed out, are of temporary, others of perpetual, obligation; none of which, however, are to be set aside except by due process and mutual agreement.

He then insisted that the clause of the Treaty of Paris, which was now under discussion, limited the sovereign rights of Russia within her own dominions. It was as if England had been bound not to fortify Portsmouth and Plymouth, and to limit her Channel Fleet to five or six small coasters. Innumerable treaties of that kind had been forced upon different European countries, and invariably they had never lasted beyond the time when the nations concerned had found themselves strong enough to throw them off. He cited the Treaty of 1815 by which France was not to allow a Bonaparte to sit upon the throne of France, and of Napoleon I casting upon the German States similar restrictions. Such treaties could not in the nature of things last, and he felt that circumstances were now such as to justify Russia in seeking for an abrogation of the Treaty of Paris by mutual conference and equitable adjustment. If, he concluded, the diplomatists of England and Russia were unable to settle such a question without flinging the whole world into war, he for one said that diplomacy was not worth its salt, and that the English taxpayer should not longer be burdened with the necessity of keeping up a useless profession.[5]

It is always difficult quite to grasp Froude's political position. His view about the Constitution is crucial to an increased understanding of it. He wrote: 'I regarded the Reformation as the grandest achievement in English history. Yet it was equally obvious that it could never have been brought about constitutionally according to modern methods. The Reformation had been the work of two powerful sovereigns, Henry VIII and Elizabeth, backed by the strongest and bravest of their subjects. To the last up to the defeat of the Armada, manhood suffrage in England would at any moment have brought back the Pope'. And that would have meant bringing back the tyrannical aspects of the Roman Catholic religion with all its political power. How does this square with Bret Hart's description of Froude as a true democrat? I believe it is best explained by his belief in the counties of England: 'English character and English freedom depend very little on the form which the Constitution assumes at Westminster'. Froude would have approved of devolution if, and only if, it meant to the 'ancient self-administered English counties'. The subject is considered at greater length in the following chapter in its relation to size and the human scale.

means the same thing in all parts of the world and that mankind equally desires it. You could not make a greater mistake. Liberty with you means that you have a right to govern yourselves, and that it is tyranny to govern. Liberty with an Asiatic means that he has a right to be governed, and that to make him govern himself is tyranny. If the people of India were your equals, you would not be here – your mission is to govern them well, or they will cut your throats.'[6]

'Cartloads of sonorous despatches from the India Office contain less wisdom than this single sentence,' commented Froude who had said something similar about the Irish in his 'Fortnight in Kerry': 'The Irish have many faults: they have one predominant virtue. There is no race in the world whose character responds more admirably to government, or suffers more injury from the absence of it.'[7]

As Dunn points out at the beginning of his chapter on Australasia: 'to do what he could to bring about a Commonwealth of English nations had become one of the ruling passions of his life,' and yet as always he wanted to define precisely the form he wanted it to take since for Froude to have a sham was worse than not to have the thing at all. Mainly I have avoided accounts of the people he met and things as he saw them in those days but one is irresistible, his meeting with Sir Henry Locke, his main host in the State of Victoria, whom he describes as 'an heroic figure who might have graced the days of Homer'. That is praise indeed and the reason for it followed: 'he had been a prisoner in the Chinese war, sentenced to be executed, and taken out every morning for a fortnight in the belief that he was to be killed there and then – a unique experience, enough in itself to have killed most men without the executioner's assistance. The composure with which he had borne the trial marked him as an exceptional person.'

Again it was characteristic of Froude that he never shied away from facing fairly and squarely anything that might run counter to his dreams, passions or reasons. He comments on the political whirl many of the Australians were in, and that included not just the important people to whom he had official introductions, but everyday people whom he always made sure to see: 'At one moment they are in a frenzy of loyalty, at the next they threaten to set up for themselves. They are very like children, but healthy, prosperous and eager, and have done miracles in covering the country with English houses. If I had Aladdin's lamp, I would empty our towns of half the squalid creatures that draggle about the gutters, and pour them out here to grow fat and rosy again.'[8]

Dunn refers to Froude's *Oceana*, his 396 page book that records his visit to Australasia, as a happy record of a happy journey. It concludes on an optimistic note but not without slipping in his own personal view of determinism. 'The event (the creation of Oceana) lies already determined, the philosophers tell us, in the chain of causation. What is to be, will be. But it is not more determined than all else which is to happen to us, and the determination does not make us sit still and wait till it comes. Among the causes are our own exertions, and each of us must do what he can, be it small or great, as this course or that seems good and right to him. If we work on the right side, coral insects as we are, we may contribute something not wholly useless to the general welfare.'[9]

And bringing *Oceana* to a conclusion he wrote:

All of us are united at present by the invisible bonds of relationship and of affection for our common country, for our common sovereign, and for our joint spiritual inheritance. These links are growing, and if let alone will continue to grow and the free fibres will of themselves become a rope of steel. A federation contrived by politicians would snap at the first strain. ... Above all, we can insist that the word 'separation' shall be no more heard among us. ... Were Oceana an accepted article of faith, received and acknowledged as something not to be called in question, it would settle into the convictions of all of us, and the organic union which we desiderate would pass silently into a fact without effort of political ingenuity. We laugh at sentiment, but every generous and living relation between man and man, or between men and their country, is sentiment and nothing else. ... And so end my observations and reflections on the dream of Sir James Harrington. So will not end, I hope and believe, Oceana.

A corollary to Froude's views on the colonies was his response to trades unions. He sympathised with the working men's petition to Queen Victoria to assist their passage to the colonies but the industrialists, those whom Ruskin called 'the black Goths', opposed it because they wanted their workmen there for the next upturn in the economy.

Froude in fact was not so starry-eyed about the Empire as many have supposed. A careful reading of his reflections as well as his writings designed to promote the idea reveals that he didn't see much else worth supporting in his own times. On his return from Australia and New Zealand he stopped at Honolulu and didn't wish to remain there for long. It prompted one of his saddest reflections, one that would run counter to his deep desire for a great confederation that would bring peace and stability to its peoples. He recorded his rather melancholy thoughts:

> I wandered about the environs looking at the people and their ways, and wondering at the nature of our Anglo-American character which was spreading us into all corners of the globe, and fashioning everything after its likeness. The original, the natural, the picturesque, goes down before it as under the wand of a magician. In the place of them springs up the commonplace and materially useful. Those who can adopt its worship and practice its liturgy, it will feed, and house, and lodge in the newest pattern; set them in a way of improving their condition by making money, of gaining useful knowledge, and enjoying themselves in tea-gardens and music-halls; while those who cannot or will not bend, it sweeps away as with the sword of a destroyer.[10]

Froude saw what he most abominated in Victorian England spreading over the world in the Anglo-American political alliance – the very opposite of the confederated Empire of his dreams in which not just the best in all the parts of the British Empire and in the end in all nations would survive and not only maintain their cultures and identities, but also manage to keep that 'percentage of scoundrels', which we all have, under control.

Just as Froude detected an evil and selfish motive in keeping the out-of-work at home with the minimum of welfare, instead of allowing them to seek a better life in the colonies, so he also saw these poor wretches as human fodder for a burgeoning trade union movement. His sympathy was, as always, with the oppressed. He longed to play his part in giving these unemployed people brighter prospects and brighter homes for their children. He saw most clearly that a nation composed of such hopeless people would soon sink in the international scale of things. He had a clear insight into the coming onslaught of what we now call globalisation. He called it intertwining: 'These are not days of small states: the natural barriers are broken down which once divided kingdom from kingdom; and with the interests of nations so much intertwined as they are now.'

He saw emigration as the only solution to the approaching impasse threatening England, the only thing that would relieve the pressure at home 'and might end the war between masters and men, and solve the problems which trades unions can only embitter'. He emphasised the point that if relations were not good between men and masters then, even in terms of the doctrine of competition, England as a country would not be able to compete with countries where they were good. His even greater fear was that England's working men would in the end turn against England itself in the way the Irish were turning against England, particular in America.

We can find money for wars, he says, but cannot find it to help people follow useful lives. He was bitter as he thought about the failure of the petition to Queen Victoria. Perhaps bitter is the wrong word. It was bitterness and its consequences that he feared. The right words might be deeply disappointed. Froude was acutely aware of the huge effect that the new means of communication were having upon the whole world. He foresaw how other nations would not be slow to copy our industrial system and that the pre-eminence of our industrial position would not last. He shared with Disraeli the view that the long-term stability of a nation depended on having a territorial foundation. Other nations had territory attached. England's were far away across the globe but Froude knew she compensated for this by being a great seafaring country. In a certain sense, Froude believed that we could recover some of the old rational government of the 18th century and perhaps something of the human scale so long as the government in Westminster refrained from making inappropriate decisions for the territories of which his great English confederation would be composed but left it to the many wise men he had met on his colonial journeys.

Chapter 6
Froude Today

The scene is Oriel College, Oxford. Anthony Froude has just arrived from London by train and he has taken a taxi to his old College where he was Regius Professor of Modern History in 1892 until he died two years later. I meet him and immediately he starts to talk about his journey down.

AF: "London has sprawled out further than we would have imagined in our day but the trains have changed very little except that they travel considerably faster and more smoothly, and there is no longer the filthy black smoke with its grey dust constantly descending at the stations. That seems to me a point in your favour but perhaps you have exchanged visible for invisible pollution and the quantity of motor driven cars I saw in London bustling about your streets – why it's worse than the horses in my day. However I hesitate to criticise. We started you off on this road and we are responsible for what you have now. When I first saw the quantity of vehicles rushing around London I imagined an anthill and supposed each of the ants to have been given a little box on wheels, in the same proportion to the ant as your er, motor cars I think you now call them – are to you. What would the result be? Would not the anthill itself grind to a halt and the ants exterminate themselves? However you seem to be getting by and

I must turn my attention to some of my other thoughts about the events that have occurred since my death at the end of the 19th century and into the 20th. I must stress that from the external perspectives events seem to have little of that urgency which you ascribe to them and which we, of course, ascribed to them in our lifetimes. No doubt you will expect me to comment on the Boer War in South Africa since I had been out there not so long beforehand and observed the situation for myself. It was surely a war which wise governments could have avoided – but governments, I'm afraid, find it very difficult to be wise since the immediate pressure of events is so great. The war itself was bad enough and was stirred up by the jingoism of the dying Victorian epoch, the motivation of nearly all wars, but it crossed my mind how terrible the consequences were going to be for South Africa, especially for the native population, as with the poor Irish peasants which I had also seen suffering on account of the folly of governments. You may think I have a bee in my bonnet about governments, but if you look around today, am I not right?"

JC: I nodded in agreement but did not wish to interrupt the flow of his comments.

AF: "I myself was now only an observer from outside this world and not as I had been in 1870 when a repetition of the Crimean debacle threatened and so I looked on with a detachment that would have been alien to me in my lifetime. I reflected on my meeting with Lord Caernarvon when he was Colonial Secretary and recalled how he hoped we might avoid the awful tragedy that was then happening. When I went out to South Africa I had hopes that the looming storm might be avoided but it was not to be so. We had talks about federation, which was quite a good word then, provided it was based on mutual goodwill. I look at the whole African continent now and all I can do is to exclaim 'Alas, poor Africa'. It is the victim of much misguided colonialism followed by misguided self-rule. I find it hard to forgive Liberal governments for their merciless disregard of their colonial responsibilities. We British had a terrible responsibility on our shoulders and we seem to exercise no greater care for the poor wretches out there, despite some very exceptional men as governors in the territories themselves, than we did for the poor wretches in our own overcrowded towns and cities. It almost seemed to me that when the Great War broke out in 1914 we were opting for killing off our surplus populations in preference to offering them a bright opportunity in the colonies where with the help sought by the Working Men's Petition they could have done much good for themselves as well as for the native peoples. How different things might have been if they had gone out with the generous help of their own country rather than as the shiploads of miserable criminals who preceded them."[1]

JC: "The Great War started so soon after the Victorian era that you must have felt that its roots were in your own times. What do you think these were?"

AF: "The killing in the Great War was on a scale that we could hardly have imagined in my time. We loved to meddle in European affairs in my day, usually to our disadvantage and in the long run usually to the disadvantage of the Continent also. Rightly used, our Royal Navy could have protected us. What would it have mattered if the German armies had reached the other side of the English Channel. It would have been a preferable no-man's land to the mud of Flanders and the other battlefields of the War. After all was said and done, only a few years earlier we had been worrying about a French invasion. I have to admit however that the loyalty of the colonies was magnificently shown – but to what purpose? Germany lost the War but a deep resentment was generated in the German people. They had to revenge their humiliation. Chancellor Hitler had no choice but to rebuild Germany with that humiliation in mind. War and preparations for war alone were the only course for a people who felt they had been cheated of victory. There was no room there for any peace with honour. It went far deeper than the Versailles Treaty.

"Another undesirable effect of the Great War was to involve America in European politics and to cause her to ignore George

Washington's emphatic warning to his countrymen never to involve themselves in European complications. From that moment when she did so entangle herself, the American Dream was transformed into a global dream such as the European imperial powers had already experienced. It is often little realised how great a part the War of Independence played in the formation of the American nation. Much is rightly made of what you call the 'Special Relationship' and I myself emphasised constantly the significance of the break with America and the foolishness of the politicians who let it happen. There was a book published earlier in the twentieth century by an American author, William Dwight Witney that has a message which we English should understand. Witney points out that: 'In their eagerness to create a national history, American writers and school-teachers have necessarily been driven to over-emphasise the early wars between the two countries ... But these two wars, entitled to so small a place in English history take a preponderant place in American school-books ... It is, unfortunately, at the youngest and most impressionable age that the normal American boy is impregnated with the idea that Britain is the hereditary enemy."[2]

JC: "Did you see signs of this problem in your time?"

AF: "Some of the colonial Governors whom I met were very resentful of some of the actions of the USA – the Canadians in particular. A great and continuous effort is needed to overcome the hidden resentments which have developed from this great misfortune in English history.

"At this point I must pursue another line of thought, partly to make my own position on Empire more clearly understood and partly as a future warning. The nineteenth century bequeathed two powerful lines of policy and action to its successor. One was an imperial policy which I myself strongly supported but with certain reservations. The other was the Liberal Party view of political economy and competition. By 'imperial policy' I meant and explicitly stated on very many occasions an English Commonwealth organised on the same basis as the old counties of England had been organised in their relations with the mother country. I was often very critical of imperial policy when it meant exercising power, often with gunboat diplomacy, around the world backed up by jingoism at home and often with a narrow view of trade that was supposed to follow the flag. I will say no more of that now but remind you of the fig tree in Natal that for my part symbolised all that I wished the British Empire to be. An Empire that only had 'interests' was of no concern to me because I knew whose interests those would be, whether achieved by free trade or by protection."

JC: "Many people in America and in the wider world have become highly critical of imperialism – in fact we hardly know where we stand in a network of 'isms' – nationalism, communism, imperialism and commercialism. We jump from one to the other as we find each leads to disastrous consequences. I suspect myself that smallism is the only one that will work."

AF: "In *Oceana* I made it clear at the end that sentiment is the basis of life: sentiment towards one another, sentiment towards our families and sentiment towards our community and towards our country. Sentiment is a delicate plant. It easily becomes embittered and turns into anti-sentiment. I remember what I once said, the exact words: 'We laugh at sentiment, but every generous and living relation between man and man and their country, is sentiment and nothing else' and I also said how children who had been nurtured in a kindly way go out into the world with a love of their family and a pride in it. The same is true of those who leave the shores of a country which has nurtured them in love. The Irish left their shores with resentment and cannot look back with pride to the country and naturally the spirit of generosity is extinguished in them.

"A country that puts its trade before its people will eventually lose the trust and natural sentiments of its people and the ultimate effect of that will plainly be to lose its trade as well. In my essay on the Reciprocal Duties of State and Subject I made this very clear. I looked at a book recently. I forget the title but I cannot forget the subtitle, 'Economics as if people mattered'.

I spent so much of my life railing against the prevailing political economy precisely because it was economics as if people didn't matter. People were referred to as 'hands': farm hands and factory hands which could be bought for money or rejected by the absence of it."

JC: "How do you explain the ambivalence in Anglo-American relations?"

AF: "My sense of the precarious basis of the relation between England and America has been partly but only partly justified. The British and American peoples on the whole have retained their loyalty to one another. Political leaders on both sides of the Atlantic may have other dreams. These will only be fully discovered by looking into the documents and letters of the times. My motives for my research into the sixteenth century was not to establish this or that fact but to gain insight into the concealed motives of the main players. You will only understand the drama of the twentieth century by doing precisely the same. I noted a couple of obvious examples. What motive did President Roosevelt have when he said that after the Second World War he would break up the British Empire and attach the pieces to the trading blocks of the world? Again I read an article in *The Times* by Sir Trevor Lloyd-Hughes, Sir Harold Wilson's Chief Information Adviser. He was with the Prime Minister at the funeral of General de Gaulle and tells how on the final morning 'Harold confided in me: "Trevor, my real deepest ambition is to become master of Europe's destiny."[3] It is scraps of information like that that actually lead to the discovery of the secret passions that actually shape the course of history."'

JC: I then asked Froude what he thought about the present state of the world.

AF: "You have it in your grasp as men have never had it before to bring total collapse to the whole of life. Somehow I believe you will avoid it. I am an optimist – but only just. I see three areas of terrifying danger: the first is the weapons you now possess which in my time would have been entirely beyond our comprehension. Nevertheless I think these are the least likely to trigger humanity's ultimate disaster. The weapons are bad enough to frighten the leaders who have the power to use them unless one of their number gets into the position of a cornered rat. This is not to say that 'weapons of mass destruction', as you call them, will not be used in limited situations as indeed they already have been.

"The second great thread of my trio comes not from science, and here I think that Mr Huxley would agree with me, but from the abuse of science. There is an enormous temptation for vested interests to manipulate science. One example is genetic engineering applied to agriculture in particular. It is very difficult to test anything adequately and it may be that the dangers lie in a more remote future and for that reason it is more likely that a wrong direction from which there is no turning back will be taken. This area also includes genetic experiments on animals and ultimately on human beings themselves.

"The third example in my trio is abuse of the environment by non-scientists, perhaps the most likely of the three to bring disaster. I know that there were developers and merchants in my day who would have taken, and in fact did take terrible risks without taking into account the effects upon the environment. Today the dangers are greatly magnified although there is a greater general awareness of them. The head of a great company will take great risks to the future of humanity if he sees the choice as being between that and the collapse of his company. This I suspect is the most likely of my trio actually to happen, although a combination of aspects of each is also quite possible.

"I did not include the morals of the people in the foregoing list because I spoke of those dangers in the future so now I turn to a danger in the forefront of the present. Unless we learn to control the barbarian inside each one of us we will find that unlike Rome of old the barbarians – some are already calling them the 'new barbarians' – are firmly within, not outside, our civilised boundaries. As in my day, politicians are short-sighted.

They are looking for votes and hardly consider the character and values of those whose support they are seeking. The votes of bad or misled people in the mass may be extremely dangerous. It is not merely a matter of the harmless deterioration of our own society that comes into question. Others outside see that something is rotten in our society and raise their voices. An example of this is to be found in Sir Richard Body's book, *England for the English*,[4] where he reproduces one of the leaflets for an Islamic rally in Trafalgar Square. We may not agree with their judgment in detail but as a whole it is a very sobering indictment: 'urban riots, suicides, alcoholism, family breakdown, child abuse, homosexuality, drug addiction, racism, poverty, unemployment and general lawlessness all bear testimony to the fact that the Western secular way of life just isn't working.' How do we answer these charges? And if we cannot answer them and the cancer in Western society grows as surely it must, a stronger society that can apply the basic rules of life will overcome us. From the earliest beginnings of man's social life on earth, government when it worked has provided the road from barbarism to civilisation. Now we are in danger of reversing the process. I shall say no more about this subject at the moment."

JC: "What is your view of the changes in the British political parties which occurred in the twentieth century?"

AF: "The growth of the Labour Party is certainly something Mr Disraeli would have approved of. It appears to have altered the balance of the political scene. The real old Conservative Party with its roots in the land and an aristocracy with an overall concern for the well being of all sections of society has gone – perhaps gone forever. Working men were to have a party that would fight for their interests against the factory owners who became the new Conservatives with all the clothing of the Liberal Party of Victorian England. Such a situation, while it might help to rectify the balance, is not tenable in the long run and can only lead to a kind of perpetual civil war. Neither side really represents England. In America it is not quite the same.

Working men's interests have been more successfully suppressed. The factory owners have won. The people have the right to fight for more and more wealth as the mighty companies entrench their political and legal power. Neither is satisfactory. Nor is it satisfactory when the working men have won the battle and leaders with no more care for the whole nation achieve a kind of dictatorship.

"While all this is going on there still are powerful players similar to Philip II in the 16th century: great bankers, great soldiers, great lawyers and, not so much in the modern world, powerful kings. Mr Disraeli expressed it in this way in one of his novels: 'So you see, my dear Coningsby, that the world is governed by very different personages from what is imagined by those who are not behind the scenes'. If it is thought that this is just the story of a mere novel, there is a very clear case in more recent times. Marcia Williams, Sir Harold Wilson's personal secretary, writes in her book *Inside No. 10* of the way in which Wilson was threatening to call an election on the question of whether we should be made to devalue the pound by Swiss bankers whom I believe he called the Gnomes of Zurich. She goes on to say how Lord Cromer, the Governor of the Bank of England, came to see Wilson and said that he could call an election and that he would win it, but 'if you do I'll break your government within six months'. The result she tells was that Wilson backed down. In my research into the archives from the sixteenth century, I was able to expose how Philip II aimed to conquer and control Europe. Today the aim is to conquer the world and the word that is used to indicate this is globalisation. I have no objection to that word but I question the way it is done in practice. If Europe is brought together in the way I pictured the British Empire under the arches of the great fig tree in Natal, how could I object? If America united its states in a similar way, and if Asia did likewise I would not complain and if these great entities became united in a world entity I can see no reason to object to that. What I warn you of is that on the road to unity at every stage there are cunning and self-deluded men waiting to take advantage of the situation, who aim to use power for their own purposes. Edmund Burke warned us that 'for evil to triumph all that is necessary is for good men to do nothing'. I would add to that. Good men must not only act but cultivate an understanding of the secret motives and passions of those who are seeking power, not for the welfare of the whole but for their own or for some sectional interest with which they have identified.

"I recently read an article in *The Times* by Sir Malcolm Rifkind, a former Foreign Secretary, in which he put forward some very interesting ideas. He suggested that both the Israelis and the Palestinians should be invited to join the Commonwealth as a step on the road to peace in the Middle East, and no doubt he meant it would have to be a Commonwealth or 'empire' on the design which I have so often described. And he added that if we really wanted to be imaginative we might invite America as well. And so we come back to *Oceana* once again in its real and true meaning.

"Sometimes in my lifetime I hoped that something of this sort might begin to be a reality. Sometimes I almost gave up hope as when I was on the shore at Haiti during my time in the West Indies. I wrote in my diary on the 30th March 1887:

I have long thought that the next great change before mankind is when sick of the commonplace, sick of towns, sick of newspapers and politics and society, sick of the detestable average of everything which levels everything to a common type, sick above all of the cant of progress and all that it means, the better part of the race will withdraw themselves into quiet homes, where they may pass their lives in quiet occupations, growing their own crops and their own fruits, may have it all pure as it used to be, and with a few good books and good engravings and their own accomplishments, which under such conditions might have real worth in them, they may save their souls, if they have any, and, if they have none, may at least spend their seventy years of existence in a manner that may bring them some real satisfaction. We seldom think on how small a stage and with how simple action all that is really interesting in the drama of human life may be played out.[5]

JC: "You've mentioned the two World Wars. What about the Cold War?"

AF: "Of course the other outstanding feature of the 20th century was the Cold War, the war in which both sides were nearly destroyed by the build-up of ghastly armaments. I suppose the savagery of two world wars was enough to restrain mankind and keep them from any further urges towards bloodshed for a while. As I viewed this strange spectacle – not so strange I suppose – of former allies turning against each other, I recalled what Sir Winston Churchill said in the days between the World Wars. He wanted to bring the Soviet Union in with Britain and France in order to check the development of Nazi Germany. He expressed the hope in Parliament that Russia would come in with us as 'A Soviet Socialist state strongly armed to maintain its national independence and absolutely divorced from any idea of spreading its doctrines abroad otherwise than by example'. I believe it would have been much better if the Communists had been forced to practice their own principles rather than being blindly opposed. Equally the Communists, had they been wise, would have done the same in reverse. Communism, like the Sabbath, was made for man, not man for Communism and the same is true for capitalism. I recall the subtitle of the book I mentioned earlier, 'Economics as if people mattered'. People, in my time, were viewed as impersonally as 'hands' to fit into an economic scheme of things and of course the same thing happens under Communism now.

"As a final point I feel constrained to defend one aspects of Carlyle's thinking. As you know he was sometimes accused of preaching a doctrine of 'might is right'. I said the reality was the exact opposite, that he saw right as the only true source of might. I shared his view of this. I believed in my time that good men needed to assert themselves if there was to be any hope of averting the day of doom and as I look upon the scene now it is just as true and even more urgent. Doom and hope are mingled as they have never been before."

And so comes to an end my interview with Anthony Froude. I join him at dinner in College and hear the theme coming up again and again in passionate discussion and on the following morning I see him to the station at Oxford on his journey to

London and Eternity – the eternity of minds which live forever. Readers may judge for themselves how well the words I put into his mouth match the words and thoughts of his essays and diaries which I quoted at length in the earlier chapters of this book.

Chapter 7

A Personal Epilogue

I hope that I have managed to present the kind of thoughts that Froude would have had if he were really here today and that what I have produced is no mere fantasy but something that his own writings fairly clearly substantiate. As I reflected on the thoughts which I ascribed to him, I wondered if there were still a few points that I myself might wish to add but which I would not be quite justified to add in his name.

Above all, I felt quite sure that he would have said that the hearts of man remain much the same in every age. Modern research seems to indicate that the genes are simply dealt out afresh in each age, a far cry from the environmentalism of the twentieth century. The king of spades and the ace of hearts are always there somewhere. The changes are usually more apparent than real and it seems to me that Froude's outlook fits in better with the 21st century than with the 20th.

I wondered about the future? It seemed to me that the great power blocs which characterised the 20th century became what they were largely because of the fear of how their neighbours would develop. The Soviet Union in the 1930s became a superpower not particularly because its leaders wanted to but because they were frightened that their country would be over-shadowed by America. No doubt it was also an excuse for them to justify their own power internally to their people. Now the European Union is justifying its development into a superpower on the grounds that it needs to act as a counterbalance to the United States. Here again fear is probably the most fundamental part of its motivation. And what of America itself? Surely the great European empires from which most of its population was made up provided ample reason for a deep-seated fear of their resurgence. Those empires have faded away but nevertheless most of the powers of Europe would follow the same route as America if the opportunities were open to them. Surely we are all going in the wrong direction. America seemed like a great new opportunity for humanity and had it followed the path that Jefferson favoured, leaving much more autonomy to the member states instead of driving in the direction of greater and greater centralisation which Hamilton supported, the world might have been a very different place. And if that had happened, would the big centralised plans of the Soviet Union ever have been realised? And were the vast collectivised farms of Russia, I wondered, an attempt to match the great wheat belts of the United States? And were their five-year plans motivated by the need to try and match the great industries of America? Some may say there is no point in all these 'what ifs' but surely this is the basis on which we have to learn from past mistakes. If we take the wrong turning when we are travelling there is a point at which our mind asks the question: 'what if I had taken the other turning'? It is the basis on which we readjust our behaviour.

My reflections took me back to the night of September 11th 2001 when I watched like millions of others the scene in New York on television, and someone who was being interviewed pointed to the collapsed towers of the World Trade Center and commented: 'that's what comes of centralising all our organisations in one place'. We are creating, I thought, a sitting duck for terrorists. If the power and organisation of America had not all been gathered up in New York and Washington and there had been 52 more or less autonomous states would the terrorists, I wondered, have known where to strike? Indeed would they have come into existence at all – as terrorists!

Here surely is a principle which applies universally? Does it not apply to Israel, for instance? The Jews, a great and ingenious people whom Froude always admired, centralised themselves in one small country, extended its boundaries and encouraged its dispersed people to migrate to it and thereby made themselves an easy target for their Arab neighbours. If instead they had kept Israel well within its post-World War II boundaries, discouraged too much immigration and worked for the fair treatment of their communities around the world, would not a better situation in the Middle East for both Jews and Arabs have been possible? Once again, perhaps, has not the chimera of power underpinned by fear attracted Israel down a fatal path from which there seems to be no escape and no prospect except for continuing disaster?

These examples lead on to thinking more about the principle of size and scale which Leopold Kohr and E.F. Schumacher, by their writings, forced the modern world to consider at a time when the prevailing view of history was that the pathway from families to tribes and from tribes to nations and to empires or superpowers was the route to higher and higher levels of civilisation. The tribal warlords frequently present an extremely unpleasant picture but even their worst excesses pale into insignificance beside what can be done with modern weapons of mass destruction, no matter how good the intentions of those who use them, and usually the tribal chiefs were at their worst when they hoped to bring some big power in on their side to crush a small neighbour as, I believe, often happened in colonial days and more recently in the conflict in Yugoslavia. Hitler, it crossed my mind, was a good example of a tribal leader who seized national power and thought he could go on to seize international power also. Froude points us in a different direction. He pointed to the traditional English counties as a true example of groups of people who had, on a small scale and over many generations, formed themselves into truly civilised entities, as opposed to societies formed rapidly by tyrants. And, incidentally, he places very little confidence in the constitution in Westminster when in a true sense it failed to represent them as did the Earl of Chatham, the elder Pitt. His words referring to the House of Commons could almost have been Froude's: 'My Lords, five hundred gentlemen are not ten millions; and if we must have a contention, let us take care to have the English nation on our side'.

Another example which Froude failed to use, perhaps deliberately, because in his day it was too closely associated with the Catholic tyranny of earlier centuries which England had escaped through the Tudor reformation of the Church, was the city states of Christian Europe in the Middle Ages. St Augustine's *City of God* was the inspiration though of course by Froude's time their days of glory had long since passed. Kohr places the following quotation from St Augustine at the heart of his *Breakdown of Nations:*

> ... the world would be most happily governed if it consisted not of a few aggregations secured by wars of conquest, with their accompaniments of despotism and tyrannic rule, but of a society of small States living together in amity, not transgressing each other's limits, unbroken by jealousies.[1]

Peter Webber in his book on the architecture of Sydney includes a wonderful description of Siena at the zenith of the civilisation of that earlier period:

> One of the most admired of cities for its urban qualities, its artistic qualities, the consistency yet variety in its public streets and places and its integrity as a total spatial composition, is the medieval city of Siena. The distinguished scholar Wolfgang Braunfels studied the thirteenth century records of town meetings to discover how that city operated at the height of its wealth and power, and how the design and alteration of its buildings and public spaces were controlled. We tend to suppose that the formal delights of the medieval city were due simply to the exquisite good taste of the ruling class and the exquisite sensibility of the medieval craftsman.
>
> Evidence of the political structure of thirteenth century Siena demonstrates otherwise. Siena was governed by a democratic assembly 'with so many separate committees that the majority of well-born citizens were occupied for the greater part of the year in the process of governing themselves and in changing the forms of

their constitution'. Each year in May a great assembly was held devoted to building and public works and from his analysis of one such assembly held in May 1297 Braunfels observed that:

'The citizens of Siena considered each project within the framework of the town as a whole. Many of the resolutions make it clear that no one was free to build at will and that very strict regulations were enforced. But from the wording of the texts, we learn that this sense of order in town planning arose from a general ideal of what a strong, beautiful and pious city should be. For the Sienese, the ordering of the town was directly connected with the order of life which, in its turn, was a mirror of the order of the Celestial City'.

Usually both the developers and the members of the town council were the influential and powerful families in the city, and all lived their lives within a kilometre or two of each other. They were the representatives of a city which was the state, and they had to live daily with the built evidence of the decisions they had made. Such direct involvement could not but breed understanding, sensitivity and heightened responsibility for their environment.

Clearly Froude believed that there was morality, security and real civilisation in small societies which had evolved over many generations. The 20th century seemed to consider that miracles could be achieved simply by the manipulation of the outer environment and had little trust in the inner forces of human nature. Froude knew that even in his day politicians relied on instant promises to establish their position and he knew also that tyrants were always waiting in the wings for opportunities which come when established governments break down or in mass democracies when people become disillusioned and lose faith in the idea of a vote that counts and means a say in the historical process. One of the most vivid examples of people looking for instant solutions and discovering terrible conse-quences was given by Julius Caesar in the Senate in 63 BC:

The Lacedaemonians, when they had conquered the Athenians, placed thirty governors over them; who began their power by putting to death, without any trial, such as were remarkably wicked and universally hated. The people were highly pleased at this, and applauded the justice of the executions. But when they had by degrees established their lawless authority, they wantonly butchered both good and bad without distinction; and thus kept the State in awe. Such was the severe punishment which the people, oppressed with slavery, suffered for their foolish joy.

It is the solid building up of government, statecraft, that can gain the genuine trust of the people that are governed and it requires both trust and patience from the people participating and the leaders alike. When that is achieved voting can and should play its part but voting in itself is no guarantee of good government or even of true democracy. People need to vote with their hearts as well as at the ballot box. Such a system requires, to use a popular phrase, building from the bottom up, from what Edmund Burke called 'the little platoons'. Above all there must be no short cuts and much pain and suffering are inevitable on the road from barbarism (which is always just below the surface of all human organisations) to civilisation. The only safeguard of human beings is good will between people and between peoples.

A final thought crosses my mind as completely appropriate to end this book. It is the question of whether smallness creates goodness or goodness creates smallness? I believe that true goodness must come first and that bigness can never come about without committing at least one of the deadly sins of the Middle Ages: Avarice. St Augustine, who has already been quoted, considered the question of size and tyranny. In Froude's day, Richard Cobden expressed a similar view in a speech in Rochdale in 1862:

> It may seem Utopian; but I don't feel sympathy for a great nation, or for those who desire the greatness of a people by the vast extension of empire. What I like to see is the growth, development, and elevation of the individual man. But we have had great empires at all times – Syria, Persia, and the rest. What trace have they left of the individual man? Nebuchadnezzar, and the countless millions under his sway, - there is no more trace of them than of herds of buffaloes, or flocks of sheep. But look at your little States; look at Greece, with its small territories, some not larger than an English county! Italy, over some of those States

a man on horseback could ride in a day, - they have left traces of individual man, where civilisation has flourished, and humanity has been elevated. It may appear Utopian, but we can never expect the individual elevated until a practical and better code of moral law prevails among nations, and until the small States obtain justice at the hands of the great.[2]

How similar to St Augustine and perhaps the most interesting feature of it is the idea of a new moral code among nations so that the large develop a new attitude towards the small. This is what has to be achieved and I think it is implied in Froude's image of the fig tree in Natal. Furthermore if that attitude prevailed in the big countries I have no doubt that their leaders would allow power to go down to the smaller units within their own structure. It seems to me that without such a moral revolution there is little hope of achieving the kind of world that I am sure the majority of ordinary people hanker after. The original American dream, the dream of their founding fathers and of the people they addressed as well as the dream of Oceana all need to become a world dream in the fast moving modern context. It would be a world without tyranny. And finally I would contrast what the Earl of Chatham had to say about Magna Carta: 'My Lords, I think that history has not done justice to their conduct, when they obtained from their sovereign that great acknowledgement of national rights contained in Magna Carta; they did not confine it to themselves alone, but delivered it as a common blessing to the whole people. ... Let us not, then, degenerate from the glorious example of our ancestors. Those iron barons (for so I may call them when compared with the silken barons of modern days) were the guardians of the people'.

Contrast this with Napoleon's remark: 'The nation is a slave that must be made to think she is on the throne'.

That Froude would have been on the side of the 'iron barons' cannot be doubted.

Appendix 1

Calvinism: An Address to the Students at St Andrew's University, Scotland, by James Anthony Froude, March 17, 1871.

Religious men, it is sometimes said, express themselves in all modes and all tenses except the present indicative. They tell us of things that were done in ancient times. They tell us of things which will be hereafter, or which might or would have been under certain conditions. Of the actual outward dispensation under which we live at present, we hear very little. The facts of experience are not sufficiently in harmony with the theories of different religious bodies to allow any sect or set of believers to appeal to them with confidence. The age of miracles is past. The world is supposed to go its own way, undisturbed by providential interferences, waiting for some final account to be taken with it hereafter; while the relations of the Creator with His creatures are confined to special and invisible process by which individual souls are saved from perdition.

Acknowledgements of this kind are no more than a tacit confession of the inadequacy of our several opinions to explain the phenomena of our lives. Results which are unapparent may be unexistent except in imagination. There is no reason to believe that the methods by which the laws of physical nature have been discovered should be inapplicable in matters of larger moment, or that the observation of facts by which alone we arrive at scientific conclusions should lead us wrong, or should lead to nothing when we interrogate them on our moral condition. Piety, like wisdom, consists in the discovery of the rules under which we are actually placed, and in faithfully obeying them. Fidelity and insight in the one case are as likely to find their reward as in the other; infidelity and blindness as likely to be answered by failure; and, in other ages, systems of religion have been vigorous and effective precisely to the extent to which they may have seen in the existing order of things the hand of a living ruler.

I may say at once that I am about to travel over serious ground. I shall not trespass on theology, though I must go near the frontiers of it. I shall give you the conclusions which I have been led to form upon a series of spiritual phenomena which have appeared successively in different ages of the world – which have exercised the most remarkable influence on the character and history of mankind, and have left their traces nowhere more distinctly than in this Scotland where we now stand.

Every one here present must have become familiar in late years with the change of tone throughout Europe and America on the subject of Calvinism. After being accepted for two centuries in all Protestant countries as the final account of the relations between man and his Maker, it has come to be regarded by liberal thinkers as a system of belief incredible in itself, dishonouring to its object, and as intolerable as it has been itself intolerant. The Catholics whom it overthrew take courage from the philosophers, and assail it on the same ground. To represent man as sent into the world under a curse, as incurably wicked – wicked by the constitution of his flesh, and wicked by eternal decree – as doomed, unless exempted by special grace which he cannot merit, or by any effort of his own obtain, to live in sin while he remains on earth, and to be eternally miserable when he leaves it – to represent him as born unable to keep the commandments, yet as justly liable to everlasting punishment for breaking them, is alike repugnant to reason and to conscience, and turns existence into a hideous nightmare. To deny the freedom of the will is to make morality impossible. To tell men that they cannot help themselves is to fling them into recklessness and despair. To what purpose the effort to be virtuous when it is an effort which is foredoomed to fail – when those that are saved are saved by no effort of their own, and confess themselves the worst of sinners, even when rescued from the penalties of sin; and those that are lost are lost by an everlasting sentence decreed against them before they were born? How are we to call the Ruler who laid under this iron code by the name of Wise, or Just, or Merciful, when we ascribe principles of action to Him which in a human father we should call preposterous and monstrous?

The discussion of these strange questions has been pursued at all times with inevitable passion, and the issue uniformly has been a drawn battle. The Arminian has entangled the Calvinist, the Calvinist has entangled the Arminian, in a labyrinth of contradictions. The advocate of free will appeals to conscience and instinct – to an *a priori* sense of what ought in equity to be. The necessitarian falls back upon the experienced reality of facts. It is true, and no argument can gainsay it, that men are placed in the world unequally favoured, both in inward disposition and outward circumstances. Some children are born with temperaments which make a life of innocence and purity natural and easy to them; others are born with violent passions, or even with distinct tendencies to evil inherited form their ancestors, and seemingly unconquerable – some are constitutionally brave, others are constitutionally cowards – some are born in religious families, and are carefully educated and watched over; others draw their first breath in an atmosphere of crime, and cease to inhale it only when they pass into their graves. Only a fourth part of mankind are born Christians. The remainder never hear the name of Christ except as a reproach. The Chinese and the Japanese – we may almost say every weaker race with whom we have come in contact – connect it only with the forced intrusion of strangers whose behaviour among them has served ill to recommend their creed. These are facts which no casuistry can explain away. And if we believe at all that the world is governed by a conscious and intelligent Being, we must believe also, however we can reconcile it with our own ideas, that these anomalies have not arisen by accident, but have been ordered of purpose and design.

No less noticeable is it that the materialistic and the metaphysical philosophers deny as completely as Calvinism what is popularly called Free Will. Every effect has its cause. In every action the will is determined by the motive which at the moment is operating most powerfully upon it. When we do wrong, we are led away by temptation, we overcome it either because we foresee inconvenient consequences, and the certainty of future pains is stronger than the present pleasure; or else because we prefer right to wrong, and our desire for good is greater than our desire for indulgence. It is impossible to conceive a man, when two courses are open to him, choosing that which he least desires. He may say that he can do what he dislikes because it is his duty. Precisely so. His desire to do his duty is a stronger motive with him than the attraction of present pleasure.

Spinoza, from entirely different premises, came to the same conclusion as Mr Mill or Mr Buckle, and can find no better account of the situation of man than in the illustration of St Paul, 'Hath not the potter power over the clay, to make one vessel to honour and another to dishonour?'

If Arminianism most commends itself to our feelings, Calvinism is nearer to the facts, however harsh and forbidding those facts may seem.

I have no intention, however, of entangling myself or you in these controversies. As little shall I consider whether men have done wisely in attempting a doctrinal solution of problems the conditions of which are so imperfectly known. The moral system of the universe is like a document written in alternate ciphers which change from line to line. We read a sentence, but at the next our key fails us; we see that there is something written there, but if we guess at it we are guessing in the dark. It seems more faithful, more becoming, in beings such as we are, to rest in the conviction of our inadequacy, and confine ourselves to those moral rules for our lives and actions on which, so far as they concern ourselves, we are left in no uncertainty at all.

At present, at any rate, we are concerned with an aspect of the matter entirely different. I am going to ask you to consider how it came to pass that if Calvinism is indeed the hard and unreasonable creed which modern enlightenment declares it to be, it has possessed such singular attractions in past times for some of the greatest men that ever lived. And how – being, as we are told, fatal to morality, because it denies free will – the first symptom of its operation, wherever it established itself, was to obliterate the distinction between sins and crimes, and to make the moral law the rule of life for States as well as persons. I shall ask you, again, why, if it is to be a creed of intellectual servitude, it was able to inspire and sustain the bravest efforts ever made by man to break the yoke of unjust authority. When all else has failed – when patriotism has covered its face and human courage has broken down – when intellect has yielded, as Gibbon says, 'with a smile or a sigh,' content to philosophise in the closet, and abroad worship with the vulgar – when emotion and sentiment and tender imaginative piety have become the handmaids of superstition, and have dreamt themselves into forgetfulness that there is any difference between lies and truth – the slavish form of belief called Calvinism, in one or other of its many forms, has borne ever an inflexible front to illusion and mendacity, and has preferred rather to be ground to powder like flint than to bend before violence, or melt under enervating temptation.

It is enough to mention the name of William the Silent, of Luther – for on the points of which I am speaking Luther was one with Calvin – of your own Knox and Andrew Melville and the Regent Murray, of Coligny, of our English Cromwell, of Milton, of John Bunyan. These were men possessed of all the qualities which give nobility and grandeur to human nature – men whose life was as upright as their intellect was commanding and their public aims untainted with selfishness; unalterably just where duty required then to be stern, but with the tenderness of a woman in their hearts; frank, true, cheerful, humorous, as unlike *sour* fanatics as it is possible to imagine any

one, and able in some way to sound the keynote to which every
brave and faithful heart in Europe instinctively vibrated.

This is the problem. Grapes do not grow on bramble-bushes.
Illustrious natures do not form themselves upon narrow and
cruel theories. Spiritual life is full of apparent paradoxes. When
St Patrick preached the Gospel on Tarah hill to Leoghaire, the
Irish kind, the Druids and the wise men of Ireland shook their
heads. 'Why,' asked the king, 'does what the cleric preaches
seem so dangerous to you?' 'Because,' was the remarkable
answer, 'because he preaches repentance, and the law of
repentance is such that a man shall say, "I may commit a
thousand crimes, and if I repent I shall be forgiven, and it will
be no worse with me: therefore I will continue to sin."' The
Druids argued logically, but they drew a false inference notwithstanding. The practical effect of a belief is the real test of its
soundness. Where we find a heroic life appearing as the
uniform fruit of a particular mode of opinion, it is childish to
argue in the face of fact that the result ought to have been
different.

The question which I have proposed, however, admits of a
reasonable answer. I must ask you only to accompany me on a
somewhat wide circuit in search of it.

There seems, in the fist place, to lie in all men, in proportion
to the strength of their understanding, a conviction that there is
in all human things a real order and purpose, notwithstanding
the chaos in which at times they seem to be involved. Suffering
scattered blindly without remedial purpose or retributive
propriety – good and evil distributed with the most absolute
disregard of moral merit or demerit – enormous crimes
perpetrated with impunity, or vengeance when it comes falling
not on the guilty but the innocent –

Desert a beggar born,
And needy nothing trimmed in jollity –

These phenomena present, generation after generation, the
same perplexing and even maddening features; and without an
illogical but none the less a positive certainty that things are not
as they seem – that, in spite of appearance, there is justice at the

heart of them, and that, in the working out of the vast drama, justice will assert somehow and somewhere its sovereign right and power, the better sort of persons would find existence altogether unendurable. This is what the Greeks meant by the Ἀνάγκη or destiny, which at the bottom is no other than moral Providence. Prometheus chained on the rock is the counterpart of Job on his dunghill. Torn with unrelaxing agony, the vulture with beak and talons rending at his heart, the Titan still defies the tyrant at whose command he suffers, and, strong in conscious innocence, appeals to the eternal Μοῖρα which will do him right in the end. The Olympian gods were cruel, jealous, capricious, malignant; but beyond and above the Olympian gods lay the silent, brooding, everlasting fate of which victim and tyrant were alike the instruments, and which at last, far off, after ages of misery it might be, but still before all was over, would vindicate the sovereignty of justice. Full as it may be of contradictions and perplexities, this obscure belief lies at the very core of our spiritual nature, and it is called fate or it is called predestination according as it is regarded pantheistically as a necessary condition of the universe, or as the decree of a self-conscious being.

Intimately connected with this belief, and perhaps the fact of which it is the inadequate expression, is the existence in nature of omnipresent organic laws, penetrating the material world, penetrating the moral world of human life and society, which insist on being obeyed in all that we do and handle – which we cannot alter, cannot modify – which will go on with us, and assist and befriend us, if we recognize and comply with them – which inexorably make themselves felt in failure and disaster if we neglect or attempt to thwart them. Search where we will among created things, far as the microscope will allow the eye to pierce, we find organization everywhere. Large forms resolve themselves into parts, but these parts are but organized after other parts, down so far as we can see into infinity. When the plant meets with the conditions which agree with it, it thrives; under unhealthy conditions it is poisoned and disintegrates. It is the same precisely with each one of ourselves, whether as individuals or as aggregated into associations, into families, into nations, into institutions. The remotest fibre of human action, from the policy of empires to the most insignificant trifle over which we waste an idle hour or moment, either moves in harmony with the true law of our being, or is else at discord with it. A king or a parliament enacts a law, and we imagine we are creating some new regulation, to encounter unprecedented circumstances. The law itself which applied to these circumstances was enacted from eternity. It has its existence independent of us, and will enforce itself either to reward or punish, as the attitude which we assume towards it is wise or unwise. Our human laws are but the copies, more or less imperfect, of the eternal laws so far as we can read them, and either succeed and promote our welfare, or fail and bring confusion and disaster, according as the legislator's insight has detected the true principle, or has been distorted by ignorance or selfishness.

And these laws are absolute, inflexible, irreversible, the steady friends of the wise and good, the eternal enemies of the blockhead and the knave. No Pope can dispense with a statute enrolled in the Chancery of Heaven or popular vote repeal it. The discipline is a stern one, and many a wild endeavour men have made to obtain less hard conditions, or imagine them other than they are. They have conceived the rule of the Almighty to be like the rule of one of themselves. They have fancied that they could bribe or appease Him – tempt Him by penance or pious offering to suspend or turn aside His displeasure. They are asking that His own eternal nature shall become other than it is. One thing only they can do. They for themselves, by changing their own courses, can make the law which they have broken thenceforward their friend. Their dispositions and nature will revive and become healthy again when they are no longer in opposition to the will of their Maker. This is the natural action of what we call repentance. But the penalties of the wrongs of the past remain unrepealed. As men have sown they must still reap. The profligate who has ruined his health or fortune may learn before he dies that he has lived as a fool, and may recover something of his peace of mind as he recovers his understanding; but no miracle takes away his paralysis, or gives back to his children the bread of which he has robbed them. He may himself be pardoned, but the consequences of his acts remain.

Once more: and it is the most awful feature of our condition. The laws of nature are general, and are no respecters of persons. There has been and there still is a clinging impression that the sufferings of men are the results of their own particular misdeeds, and that no one is or can be punished for the faults of others. I shall not dispute about the word 'punishment'. 'The fathers have eaten sour grapes,' said the Jewish proverb, 'and the children's teeth are set on edge.' So said Jewish experience, and Ezekiel answered that these words should no longer be used among them. 'The soul that sinneth, it shall die.' Yes, there is a promise that the soul shall be saved, there is no such promise for the body. Every man is the architect of his own character, and if to the extent of his opportunities he has lived purely, nobly and uprightly, the misfortunes which may fall on him through the crimes or errors of other men cannot injure the immortal part of him. But it is no less true that we are made dependent one upon another to a degree which can hardly be exaggerated. The winds and waves are on the side of the best navigator – the seaman who best understands them. Place a fool at the helm, and crew and passengers will perish, be they ever so innocent. The Tower of Siloam fell, not for any sins of the eighteen who were crushed by it, but through bad mortar probably, the rotting of a beam, or the uneven settling of the foundations. The persons who should have suffered, according to our notions of distributive justice, were the ignorant architects or masons who had dome their work amiss. But the guilty had perhaps long been turned to dust. And the law of gravity brought the tower down at its own time, indifferent to the persons who might be under it.

Now the feature which distinguishes man from other animals is that he is able to observe and discover these laws which are of such mighty moment to him, and direct his conduct in conformity with them. The more subtle may be revealed only by complicated experience. The plainer and more obvious – among those especially – have been apprehended among the higher races easily and readily. I shall not ask how the knowledge of them has been obtained, whether by external revelation, or by natural insight, or by some other influence working through human faculties. The fact is all that we are concerned with, that from the earliest times of which we have historical knowledge there have always been men who have recognised the distinction between the nobler and baser parts of their being. They have perceived that if they would be men and not beasts, they must control their animal passions, prefer truth to falsehood, courage to cowardice, justice to violence, and compassion to cruelty. These are the elementary principles of morality, on the recognition of which the welfare and improvement of mankind depend, and human history has been little more than a record of the struggle which began at the beginning and will continue to the end between the few who have had ability to see into the truth and loyalty to obey it, and the multitude who by evasion or rebellion have hoped to thrive in spite of it.

Thus we see that in the better sort of men there are two elementary convictions; that there is over all things an unsleeping, inflexible, all-ordering, just power, and that this power governs the world by laws which can be seen in their effects, and on the obedience to which, and on nothing else, human welfare depends.

And now I will suppose some one whose tendencies are naturally healthy, though as yet no special occasions shall have roused him to serious thought, growing up in a civilized community, where, as usually happens, a compromise has been struck between vice and virtue, where a certain difference between right and wrong is recognized decently on the surface, while below it one-half of the people are rushing steadily after the thing called pleasure, and the other half labouring in drudgery to provide the means of it for the idle.

Of practical justice in such a community there will be exceedingly little, but as society cannot go along at all without paying morality some outward homage, there will of course be an established religion – an Olympus, a Valhalla, or some system of theogony or theology, with temples, priests, liturgies, public confessions in one form or another of the dependence we see upon what is not seen, with certain ideas of duty and penalties imposed for neglect of it. These there will be, and also, as obedience is disagreeable and requires abstinence from various indulgences, there will be contrivances by which indulgences can be secured, and no harm come of it. By the side of the moral law there grows up a law of ceremonial observance, to which is attached a notion of superior sanctity and especial obligation. Morality, though not at first disowned, is slighted as comparatively trivial. Duty in the high sense comes to mean religious duty, that is to say, the attentive observance of certain forms and ceremonies, and these forms and ceremonies come into collision little or not at all with ordinary life, and ultimately have a tendency to resolve themselves into payments of money.

Thus rises what is called idolatry. I do not mean by idolatry the mere worship of manufactured images. I mean the separation between practical obligation, and new moons and sabbaths, outward acts of devotion, or formulas of particular opinions. It is a state of things perpetually recurring; for there is nothing, if it would only act, more agreeable to all parties concerned. Priests find their office magnified and their consequence increased. Laymen can be in favour with God and man, so priests will tell them, while their enjoyments or occupations are in no way interfered with. The mischief is that the laws of nature remain meanwhile unsuspended; and all the functions of society become poisoned through neglect of them. Religion, which ought to have been a restraint, becomes a fresh instrument of evil – to the imaginative and the weak a con-temptible superstition, to the educated a mockery, to knaves and hypocrites a cloak of iniquity, to all alike – to those who suffer and those who seem to profit by it – a lie so palpable as to be worse than atheism itself.

There comes a time when all this has to end. The over-indulgence of the few is the over-penury of the many. Injustice begets misery, and misery resentment. Something happens perhaps – some unusual oppression, or some act of religious mendacity especially glaring. Such a person as I am supposing asks himself, 'What is the meaning of these things?' His eyes are opened. Gradually he discovers that he is living surrounded with falsehood, drinking lies like water, his conscience polluted, his intellect degraded by the abominations which envelope his existence. At first perhaps he will feel most keenly for himself. He will not suppose that he can set to rights a world that is out of joint, but he will himself relinquish his share in what he detests and despises. He withdraws into himself. If what others are doing and saying is obviously wrong, then he has to ask himself what is right, and what is the true purpose of his existence. Light breaks more clearly on him. He becomes conscious of impulses towards something purer and higher than he has yet experienced or even imagined. Whence these impulses come he cannot tell. He is too keenly aware of the selfish and cowardly thoughts which rise up to mar and thwart his nobler aspirations, to believe that they can possibly be his own. If he conquers his baser nature he feels that he is conquering himself. The conqueror and the conquered cannot be the same; and he therefore concludes, not in vanity, but in profound humiliation and self-abasement, that the infinite grace of God and nothing else is rescuing him from destruction. He is converted, as the theologians say. He sets his face upon another road from that which he has hitherto travelled, and to which he can never return. It has been no merit of his own. His disposition will rather be to exaggerate his own worthlessness, that he may exalt his own worthlessness, that he may exalt the more what has been done for him, and he resolves thenceforward to enlist himself as a soldier on the side of truth and right, and to have no wishes, no desires, no opinions but what the service of his Master imposes. Like a soldier he abandons his freedom, desiring only like a soldier to act and speak as of himself, but as commissioned from some supreme authority. In such a condition a man becomes magnetic. There are epidemics of nobleness as well as epidemics of disease; and he infects others with his own enthusiasm. Even in the most corrupt ages there are always more persons than we suppose who in their hearts rebel against the prevailing fashions; one takes courage from another; communities form themselves with higher principles of action and purer intellectual beliefs. As their numbers multiply they catch fire with a common idea and a common indignation, and ultimately burst out into open war with the lies and iniquities that surround them.

I have been describing a natural process which has repeated itself many times in human history, and, unless the old opinion that we are more than animated clay, and that our nature has nobler affinities, dies away into a dream, will repeat itself at recurring intervals, so long as our race survives upon the planet.

I have told you generally what I conceive to be our real position, and the administration under which we live; and I have indicated how naturally the conviction of the truth would tend to express itself in the moral formulas of Calvinism. I will now run briefly over the most remarkable of the great historical movements to which I have alluded; and you will see, in the striking recurrence of the same peculiar mode of thought and action, an evidence that, if not completely accurate, it must possess some near and close affinity with the real fact. I will take first the example with which we are all most familiar – that of the chosen people. I must again remind you that I am not talking of theology. I say nothing of what is called technically revelation. I am treating these matters as phenomena of human experience, the lessons of which would be identically the same if no revelation existed.

The discovery of the key to the hieroglyphics, the excavations in the tombs, the investigations carried on by a series of careful inquirers, from Belzoni to Lepsius, into the antiquities of the Valley of the Nile, interpreting and in turn interpreted by Manetho and Herodotus, have thrown a light in many respects singularly clear upon the condition of the first country which, so far as history can tell, succeeded in achieving a state of high civilization. From a period the remoteness of which it is unsafe to conjecture there had been established in Egypt an elaborate and splendid empire, which, though it had not escaped revolutions, had suffered none which had caused organic changes there. It had strength, wealth, power, coherence, a vigorous monarchy, dominant and exclusive castes of nobles and priests, and a proletariat of slaves. Its cities, temples, and monuments are still, in their ruin, the admiration of engineers, and the despair of architects. Original intellectual conceptions inspired its public buildings. Saved by situation, like China, from the intrusion of barbarians, it developed at leisure its own ideas, undisturbed from without; and when it becomes historically visible to us it was in the zenith of its glory. The habits of the higher classes were elaborately luxurious, and the vanity and the self-indulgence of the few were made possible – as it is and always must be where vanity and self-indulgence exist – by the oppression and misery of the millions. You can see on the sides of the tombs – for their pride and their pomp followed them even in their graves – the effeminate patrician of the court of the Pharaohs reclining in his gilded gondola, the attendant eunuch waiting upon him with the goblet or plate of fruit, the bevies of languishing damsels fluttering round him in their transparent draperies. Shakespeare's Cleopatra might have sat for the portrait of the Potiphar's wife who tried the virtue of the son of Jacob:

> The barge she sate in, like a burnished throne,
> Burned on the water: the poop was beaten gold;
> Purple the sails, and so perfumed that
> The winds were love-sick with them. ...
> > For her own person,
> It beggared all description: she did lie
> In her pavilion – cloth-of-gold of tissue –
> O'er-picturing that Venus where we see
> The fancy out-work nature: on each side her
> Stood pretty dimpled boys, like smiling Cupids,
> With divers-coloured fans, whose wind did seem
> To glow the delicate cheeks which they did cool,
> And what they did, undid.

By the side of all this there was a no less elaborate religion – an ecclesiastical hierarchy – powerful as the sacerdotalism of Mediaeval Europe, with a creed in the middle of it which was a complicated idolatry of the physical forces.

There are at bottom but two possible religions – that which rises in the moral nature of man, and which takes shape in

moral commandments, and that which grows out of the observations of the material energies which operate in the external
universe. The sun at all times has been the central object of this
material reverence. The sun was the parent of light; the sun was
the lord of the sky and the lord of the seasons; at the sun's
bidding the earth brought forth her harvests and ripened them
to maturity. The sun, too, was beneficent to the good and to the
evil, and, like the laws of political economy, drew no harsh dis-
tinctions between one person and another – demanding only
that certain work should be done, and smiling equally in the
crops of the slave-driver and the garden of the innocent
peasant. The moon, when the sun sunk to his night's rest,
reigned as his vice-regent, the queen of the revolving heavens,
and in her waxing and waning and singular movement among
the stars was the perpetual occasion of admiring and adoring
curiosity. Nature in all her forms was wonderful; nature in her
beneficent forms was to be loved and worshipped; and being, as
Nature is, indifferent to morality, bestowing prosperity on
principles which make no demands on chastity or equity, she is,
in one form or other, the divinity at whose shrine in all ages the
favoured sections of society have always gladly made their
homage. Where Nature is sovereign, there is no need of
austerity and self-denial. The object of life is the pursuit of
wealth and pleasures which wealth can purchase; and the rules
for our practical guidance are the laws, as the economists say, by
which wealth can be acquired.

It is an excellent creed for those who have the happiness to
profit by it, and will have its followers to the end of time. In
these later ages it connects itself with the natural sciences,
progress of the intellect, specious shadows of all kinds which
will not interfere with its supreme management of political
arrangements. In Egypt, where knowledge was in its
rudiments, every natural force, the minutest plant and animals,
which influenced human fortunes for good or evil, came in for
a niche in the shrine of the temples of the sun and moon.
Snakes and crocodiles, dogs, cats, cranes, and beetles were
propitiated by sacrifices, by laboured ceremonials of laudation;
nothing living was too mean to find a place in the omnivorous

devotionalism of the Egyptian clergy. We, in these days, proud as we may be of our intellectual advances, need not ridicule popular credulity. Even here in Scotland, not so long ago, wretched old women were supposed to run about the country in the shape of hares. At this very hour the ablest of living natural philosophers is looking gravely to the courtship of moths and butterflies to solve the problem of the origin of man, and prove his descent from an African baboon.

There was, however, in ancient Egypt another article of faith besides nature-worship of transcendent moment – a belief which had probably descended from earlier and purer ages, and had then originated in the minds of sincere and earnest men – as a solution of the real problem of humanity. The inscriptions and paintings in the tombs near Thebes make it perfectly clear that the Egyptians looked forward to a future state – to the judgment-bar of Osiris, where they would each one day stand to give account for their actions. They believed as clearly as we do, and with a conviction of a very similar kind, that those who had done good would go to everlasting life, and those who had done evil into eternal perdition.

Such a belief, if coupled with an accurate perception of what good and evil mean – with a distinct certainty that men will be tried by the moral law, before a perfectly just judge, and that no subterfuges will avail. – cannot but exercise a most profound and most tremendous influence upon human conduct. And yet our own experience, if nothing else, proves that this belief, when moulded into traditional and conventional shapes, may lose its practical power; nay, without ceasing to be professed, and even sincerely held, may become more mischievous than salutary. And this is owing to the fatal distinction of which I spoke just now, which seems to have an irresistible tendency to shape itself, in civilized societies, between religious and moral duties. With the help of this distinction it becomes possible for a man, as long as he avoids gross sins, to neglect every one of his positive obligations – to be careless, selfish, unscrupulous, indifferent to everything but his own pleasures – and to imagine all the time that his condition is perfectly satisfactory, and that he can look forward to what is before him without the slightest uneasiness. All accounts represent the Egyptians as an eminently religious people. No profanity was tolerated there, no scepticism, no insolent disobedience to the established priesthood. If a doubt ever crossed the mind of some licentious philosopher as to the entire sacredness of the stainless Apis, if ever a question forced itself on him whether the Lord of heaven and earth could really be incarnated in the stupidest of created beasts, he kept his counsels to himself, if he was not shocked at his own impiety. The priests, who professed supernatural powers – the priests, who were in communication with the gods themselves – they possessed the keys of the sacred mysteries, and what was Philosophy that it should lift its voice against them? The word of the priest – nine parts a charlatan, and one part, perhaps, himself imposed on – was absolute. He knew the counsels of Osiris, he knew that the question which would be asked at the dread tribunal was not whether a man had been just and true and merciful, but whether he had believed what he was told to believe, and had duly paid the fees to the temple. And so the world went its way, controlled by no dread of retributions; and on the tomb-frescoes you can see legions of slaves under the lash dragging from the quarries the blocks of granite which were to form the eternal monuments of the Pharaohs' tyranny; and you read in the earliest authentic history that when there was a fear that the slave-races should multiply so fast as to be dangerous their babies were flung to the crocodiles.

One of these slave-races rose at last in revolt. Noticeably it did not rise against oppression as such, or directly in consequence of oppression. We hear of no massacre of slave-drivers, no burning of towns or villages, none of the usual accompaniments of peasant insurrections. If Egypt was plagued, it was not by mutinous mobs or incendiaries. Half a million men simply rose up and declared that they could endure no longer the mendacity, the hypocrisy, the vile and incredible rubbish which was offered to them in the sacred name of religion. 'Let us go,' they said, into the wilderness, go out of these soft water-meadows and corn-fields, forsake our leeks and our flesh-pots, and take in exchange a life of hardship and wandering, 'that we may worship the God of our fathers.' Their leader had been trained in the wisdom of the Egyptians, and among the rocks of Sinai had learnt that it was wind and vanity. The half-obscured traditions of his ancestors awoke to life again, and were rekindled by him in his people. They would bear with lies no longer. They shook the dust of Egypt from their feet, and the prate and falsehood of it from their souls, and they withdrew, with all belonging to them, into the Arabian desert, that they might no longer serve cats and dogs and bulls and beetles, but the Eternal Spirit who had been pleased to make his existence known to them. They sung no paean of liberty. They were delivered from the house of bondage, but it was a bondage of mendacity, and they left it only to assume another service. The Eternal had taken pity on them. In revealing his true nature to them, he had taken them for his children. They were not their own, but his, and they laid their lives under commandments which were as close a copy as, with the knowledge which they possessed, they could make, to the moral laws of the Maker of the universe. In essentials the Book of the Law was a covenant of practical justice. Rewards and punishments were alike immediate, both to each separate person and to the collective nation. Retribution in a life to come was dropped out of sight, but not insisted on. The belief that it had been corrupted to evil, and rather enervated than encouraged the efforts after present equity. Every man was to reap as he had sown – here, in the immediate world – to live under his own vine and fig-tree, and thrive or suffer according to his actual deserts. Religion was not a thing of the past or future, and account of things that had been, or of things which one day would be again. God was the actual living ruler of real every-day life; nature-worship was swept away, and in the warmth and passion of conviction they became, as I said, the soldiers of a purer creed. In Palestine, where they found idolatry in a form yet fouler and more cruel than what they had left behind them, they trampled it out as if in inspired abomination of a system of which the fruits were so detestable. They were not perfect – very far from perfect. An army at best is made of mixed materials, and war, of all ways of making wrong into right is the harshest; but they were directed by a noble purpose, and they have left a mark never to be effaced in the history of the human race.

The fire died away. 'The Israelites,' we are told, 'mingled among the heathen and learned their works.' They ceased to be missionaries. They hardly and fitfully preserved the records of the meaning of their own exodus. Eight hundred years went by and the flame rekindled in another country. Cities more splendid than the hundred-gated Thebes itself had risen on the banks of the Euphrates. Grand military empires had followed when no enemies were left to conquer; and with peace had come philosophy, science, agricultural enterprise, magnificent engineering works for the draining and irrigation of the Mesopotamian plains. Temples and palaces towered into the sky. The pomp and luxury of Asia rivalled, and even surpassed, the glories of Egypt; and by the side of it a second nature-worship, which, if less elaborately absurd, was more deeply detestable. The foulest vices were consecrated to the service of the gods, and the holiest ceremonies inoculated with impunity and sensuality.

The seventh century before the Christian era was distinguished over the whole East by extraordinary religious revolutions. With the most remarkable of these, that which bears the name of Buddha, I am not here concerned. Buddhism has been the creed for more than two thousand years of half the human race, but it left unaffected our own western world, and therefore I here pass it by.

Simultaneously with Buddha there appeared another teacher, Zerdusht, or, as the Greeks called him, Zoroaster, among the hardy tribes of the desert mountains. He taught a creed which, like that of the Israelites, was essentially moral and extremely simple. Nature-worship, as I said, knew nothing of morality. When the objects of natural idolatry became personified, and physical phenomena were metamorphosed into allegorical mythology, the indifference to morality, which was obvious in nature, became ascribed as a matter of course to gods which were but nature in a personal disguise. Zoroaster, like Moses, saw behind the physical forces into the deeper laws of right and wrong. He supposed himself to discover two antagonist powers, contending in the heart of man as well as in the outward universe – a spirit of falsehood, a spirit life-giving and beautiful, a spirit poisonous and deadly. To one or other of these powers man was necessarily in servitude. As the follower of Ormuzd, he became enrolled in the celestial armies, whose business was to fight against wrong-doing and impurity, against injustice and lies and baseness of all sorts and kinds; and every one with a soul in him to prefer good to evil was summoned to the holy wars, which would end at last after ages in the final overthrow of Ahriman.

The Persians caught rapidly Zoroaster's spirit. Uncorrupted by luxury, they responded eagerly to a voice which they recognized as speaking truth to them. They have been called the Puritans of the Old World. Never any people, it is said, hated idolatry as they hated it, and for the simple reason that they hated lies. A Persian lad, Herodotus tells us, was educated in three especial accomplishments. He was taught to ride, to shoot, and to speak the truth – that is to say, he was brought up to be brave, active, valiant and upright. When a man speaks the truth, you may count pretty surely that he possesses most other virtues. Half the vices in the world rise out of cowardice, and one who is afraid of lying is usually afraid of nothing else. Speech is an article of trade in which we are all dealers, and the one beyond all others where we are most bound to provide honest wares:

ἐχθρός μοι κἀκεῖνος ὁμῶς Ἀΐδαο πυλαῖσιν ὅς θ' ἑτερόν μεν κεύθῃ ἐνὶ φρέσιν ἄλλο δὲ εἴπῃ.

Hateful to me like the Gates of Hell is the man who hides one thing in his heart and says another.

Homer, *Iliad* 9 312-3

This seems to have been the Persian temperament, and in virtue of it they were chosen as the instruments – clearly recognised as such by the Prophet Isaiah for one – which were to sweep the earth clean of abominations, which had grown to an intolerable height. Bel bowed down, and Nebo had to stoop before them. Babylon, the lady of kingdoms, was laid in the dust, and 'her star-gazers and her astrologers and her monthly prognosticators' could not save her with all their skill. They and she were born away together. Egypt's turn followed. Retribution had been long delayed, but her cup ran over at last. The palm-groves were flung into the river, the temples polluted, the idols mutilated. The precious Apis, for all its godhead, was led with a halter before the Persian king, and stabbed in the sight of the world by Persian steel.

'Profane!' exclaimed the priests, as pious persons, on like occasions, have exclaimed a thousand times: 'these Puritans have no reverence for holy things.' Rather it is because they do reverence things which deserve reverence that they loathe and abhor the counterfeit. What does an ascertained imposture deserve but to be denied, exposed, insulted, trampled under-foot, danced upon, if nothing less will serve, till the very geese take courage and venture to hiss derision? Are we to wreathe aureoles round the brows of phantasms lest we shock the sensibilities of the idiots who have believed them to be divine? Was the Prophet Isaiah so tender in his way of treating such matters?

> Who hath formed a god, or molten a graven image that is profitable for nothing? He heweth him down cedars. He taketh the cypress and the oak from the trees of the forest. He burneth part thereof in the fire; with part thereof he eateth flesh. He roasteth roast, and is satisfied: yea, he warmeth himself, and saith, Aha, I am warm, I have seen the fire: and the residue thereof he maketh a god, even his graven image: he falleth down unto it, and worshippeth it, and prayeth unto it, and saith, Deliver me; for thou art my god.
>
> Enter into the rock, and hide thee in the dust, for fear of the Lord, for the glory of His majesty when he ariseth to shake terribly the earth. In that day a man shall cast his idols of silver and gold, which they made each one for himself to worship, to the moles and the bats.

Again events glide on. Persian runs the usual course. Virtue and truth produced strength, strength dominion, dominion riches, riches luxury, and luxury weakness and collapse – fatal sequence repeated so often, yet to so little purpose. The hardy warrior of the mountains degenerated into a vulgar sybarite. His manliness became effeminacy; his piety a ritual of priests;

himself a liar, a coward, and a slave. The Greeks conquered the Persians, copied their manners, and fell in turn before the Romans. We count little more than 500 years from the fall of Babylon, and the entire known world was lying at the feet of a great military despotism. Coming originally themselves from the East, the classic nations had brought with them also the primaeval nature-worship of Asia. The Greek imagination had woven the Eastern metaphors into a singular mythology, in which the gods were represented as beings possessing in a splendid degree physical beauty, physical strength, with the kind of awfulness which belonged to their origin; the fitful, wanton, changeable, yet also terrible powers of the elemental world. Translated into the language of humanity, the actions and adventures thus ascribed to the gods became in process of time impossible to be believed. Intellect expanded; moral sense grew more vigorous, and with it the conviction that if the national traditions were true man must be more than just his Maker. In Aeschylus and Sophocles, in Pindar and Plato, you see conscience asserting its sovereignty over the most sacred beliefs – instinctive reverence and piety struggling sometimes to express themselves under the names and forms of the past, sometimes bursting out uncontrollably into indignant abhorrence:

> To me 'twere strange indeed
> To charge the blessed gods with greed,
> I dare not do it. …
> Myths too oft,
> With quaintly coloured lies enwrought,
> To stray from the truth have mortals brought.
> And art, which round all things below
> A charm of loveliness can throw,
> Has robed the false in honour's hue,
> And made the incredible seem true.

'All religions,' says Gibbon, 'are to the vulgar equally true, to the philosopher equally false, and to the statesman equally useful:' thus scornfully summing up the theory of the matter which he found to be held by the politicians of the age which he was describing, and perhaps of his own. Religion, as a moral force, died away with the establishment of the Roman Empire, and with it died probity, patriotism, and human dignity, and all that men had learnt in nobler ages to honour and to value as good. Order reigned unbroken under the control of the legions. Industry flourished, and natural science, and most of the elements of what we now call civilization. Ships covered the seas. Huge towns adorned the Imperial provinces. The manners of men became more artificial, and in a certain sense more humane. Religion was a State establishment – a decent acknowledgement of a power or powers which, if they existed at all, amused themselves in the depths of space, careless, so their deity was not denied, of the woe or weal of humanity: the living fact, supreme in Church and State, being the wearer of the purple, who, as the practical realization of authority, assumed the name as well as the substance. The one god immediately known to man was thenceforth the Divus Caesar, whose throne in the sky was waiting empty for him to join or rejoin his kindred divinities.

It was the era of atheism – atheism such as this earth never witnessed before or since. You who have read Tacitus know the practical fruits of it, as they appeared at the heart of the system in the second Babylon, the proud city of the seven hills. You will remember how, for the crime of a single slave, the entire household of a Roman patrician, four hundred innocent human beings, were led in chains across the Forum and murdered by what was called law. You will remember the exquisite Nero, who, in his love of art, to throw himself more fully into the genius of Greek tragedy, committed incest with his mother that he might realize the sensations of Orestes. You will recall one scene which Tacitus describes, not as exceptional or standing alone, but merely, he says, 'quas ut exemplum refeream be saepius eadem prodigentia narranda sit' – the hymeneal night-banquet on Agrippa's lake, graced by the presence of the wives and daughters of the Roman senators, where amidst blazing fireworks and music and cloth-of-gold pavilions and naked prostitutes, the majesty of the Caesars celebrated his nuptials with a boy.

There, I conceive, was the visible product of material civilization, where there was no fear of God in the middle of it – the final outcome of wealth and prosperity and art and culture, raised aloft as a sign for all ages to look upon.

But it is not to this, nor to the fire of hell which in due time burst out to consume it, that I desire now to draw your attention. I have to point out to you two purifying movements which were at work in the midst of the pollution, one of which came to nothing and survives only in books, the second a force which was to mould for ages the future history of man. Both require our notice, for both singularly contained the particular feature which is called the reproach of Calvinism.

The blackest night is never utterly dark. When mankind seem most abandoned there are always a seven thousand somewhere who have not bowed the knee to the fashionable opinions of the hour. Among the great Roman families a certain number remained republican in habit. The State religion was as incredible to them as to every one else. They could not persuade themselves that they could discover the will of Heaven in the colour of a calf's liver or in the appetite of the sacred chickens; but they had retained the moral instincts of their citizen ancestors. They knew nothing of God or the gods, but they had something in themselves which made sensuality nauseating instead of pleasant to them. They had an austere sense of the meaning of the word 'duty'. They could distinguish and reverence the nobler possibilities of their nature. They disdained what was base and effeminate, and, though religion failed them, they constructed out of philosophy a rule which would serve to live by. Stoicism is not unnatural refuge of thoughtful men in confused and sceptical ages. It adheres rigidly to morality. It offers no easy Epicurean explanation of the origin of man, which resolves him again into nothingness. It recognizes only that men who are the slaves of their passions are miserable and impotent, and insists that personal inclinations shall be subordinated to conscience. It prescribes plainness of life, that the number of our necessities may be as few as possible; and in placing the business of life in intellectual and moral action it destroys the temptation to sensual gratifications. It teaches a contempt of death so complete that it can be encountered without a flutter of the pulse; and while it raises men above the suffering which makes others miserable, generates a proud submissiveness to sorrow which noblest natures feel most keenly, by representing this huge scene and the shows which it presents as the work of some unknown but irresistible force, against which it is vain to struggle and childish to repine.

As with Calvinism, a theoretic belief in an overruling will or destiny was not only compatible with but seemed natural to issue in the control of the animal appetites. The Stoic did not argue that, 'as fate governs all things, I can do no wrong, and therefore I will take my pleasure:' but rather, 'The moral law within me is the noblest part of my being and compels me to submit to it'. He did not withdraw from the world like the Christian anchorite. He remained at his post in the senate, the Forum, or the army. A Stoic in Marcus Aurelius gave a passing dignity to the dishonoured purple. In Tacitus, Stoicism has left an external evidence how grand a creature man may be, though unassisted by conscious dependence on external spiritual help, through steady disdain of what is base, steady reverence for all that deserves to be revered, and inflexible integrity in word and deed.

But Stoicism could under no circumstances be a regenerating power in the general world. It was a position only tenable to the educated; it was without hope and without enthusiasm. From a contempt of the objects which mankind most desired, the step was short and inevitable to contempt of mankind themselves. Wrapped in mournful self-dependence, the Stoic could face calmly for himself whatever lot the fates might send:

Si fractus illabatur orbis,
Impavidum ferient ruinae.

But, natural as such a creed be in a Roman noble under the Empire, natural perhaps as it may always be in corrupted ages and amidst disorganised beliefs, the very sternness of Stoicism was repellent. It carried no consolation to the hearts of the suffering millions, who were in no danger of being led away by luxury, because their whole lives were passed in poverty and wretchedness. It was individual, not missionary. The Stoic declared no active war against corruption. He stood alone, protesting scornfully in silent example against evils which he was without power to cure. Like Caesar, he folded himself in his mantle. The world might do its worst. He would keep his own soul unstained.

Place beside the Stoics their contemporaries the Galilean fishermen and the tent-maker of Tarsus. I am not about to sketch in a few paragraphs the rise of Christianity. I mean only to point to the principles on which the small knot of men gathered themselves together who were about to lay the foundations of a vast spiritual revolution. The guilt and wretchedness in which the world was steeped St Paul felt as keenly as Tacitus, Like Tacitus, too, he believed that the wild and miserable scene which he beheld was no result of accident, but had been ordained so to be, and was the direct expression of an all-mastering Power. But he saw also this Power was no blind necessity or iron chain of connected cause and effect, but a perfectly just, perfectly wise being, who governed all things by the everlasting immutable laws of his own nature; that when these laws were resisted or forgotten they wrought ruin and confusion and slavery to death and sin; that when they recognized and obeyed the curse would be taken away, and freedom and manliness come back again. Whence the disobedience had first risen was a problem which St Paul solved in a manner not at all unlike the Persians. There was a rebellious spirit in the universe, penetrating into men's hearts, and prompting them to disloyalty and revolt. It removed the question a step further back without answering it, but the fact was plain as the sunlight. Men had neglected the laws of their Maker. In neglecting them they had brought universal ruin, not on themselves only, but on all society, and if the world was to be saved from destruction they must be persuaded or forced back into their allegiance. The law itself has been once more revealed on the mountains of Palestine, and in the person and example of one who had lived and died to make it known; and those who had heard and known Him, being possessed with His spirit, felt themselves commissioned as a missionary legion to publish the truth to mankind. They were not, like the Israelites or the Persians, to fight with the sword – not even in their own defence. The sword can take life, but not give it; and the command to the Apostles was to sow the invisible seed in the hotbed of corruption, and feed and foster it, and water it, with the blood not of others, but themselves. Their own wills, ambitions, hopes, desires, emotions, were swallowed up in the will to which they had surrendered themselves. They were soldiers. It was St Paul's metaphor, and no other is so appropriate. They claimed no merit through their calling; they were too conscious of their own sins to indulge in the poisonous reflection that they were not as other men. They were summoned out on their allegiance, and armed with the spiritual strength which belongs to the consciousness of a just cause. If they indulged any personal hope, it was only that their weaknesses would not be remembered against them – that, having been chosen for a work in which the victory was assured, they be made themselves worthy of their calling, and, though they might slide, would not be allowed to fall. Many mysteries remained unsolved. Man was as clay in the potter's hand – one vessel was made to honour and another to dishonour. Why, who could tell? This only they knew, that they must themselves do no dishonour to the spirit that was in them – gain others, gain all who would join them for their common purpose, and fight with all their souls against ignorance and sin.

The fishermen of Gennesaret planted Christianity, and many a winter and many a summer have since rolled over it. More than once it has shed its leaves and seemed to be dying, and when the buds burst again the colour of the foliage was changed. The theory of it which is taught to-day in the theological schools of St Andrew's would have sounded strange from the pulpit of your once proud cathedral. As the same thought expresses itself in many languages, so spiritual truths can assume ever-varying forms. The garment fades – the moths devour it – the woven fibres disintegrate and turn to dust. The idea only is immortal, and never fades. The hermit who made his cell below the cliff where the cathedral stands, the monkish architect who designed the plan of it, the princes who brought it to perfection, the Protestants who shattered it into ruin, the preacher of last Sunday at the University church, would have many a quarrel were they to meet now before they would understand each other. But at the bottom of the minds of all the same thought would be predominant – that they were soldiers of the Almighty, commissioned to fight with lies and selfishness, and that all alike, they and those against whom they were contending, were in his hands, to deal with after his own pleasure.

Again six centuries go by. Christianity becomes the religion of the Roman Empire. The Empire divides, and the Church is divided with it. Europe is overrun by the Northern nations. The power of the Western Caesars breaks in pieces, but the Western Church stands erect, makes its way into the hearts of the conquerors, penetrates the German forests, opens a path into Britain and Ireland. By the noble Gothic nations it is welcomed with passionate enthusiasm. The warriors of Odin are transformed into a Christian chivalry, and the wild Valhalla into a Christian Heaven. Fiery passionate nations are not tamed in a generation or a century, but a new conception of what was praiseworthy and excellent had taken hold of their imagination and their understanding. Kings, when their day of toil was over, laid down crown and sword, and retired into cloisters, to pass what remained of life to them in prayers and meditations on eternity. The supreme object of reverence was no longer the hero of the battle-field, but the barefoot missionary who was carrying the Gospel among the tribes that were still untaught. So beautiful in their conception of him was the character of one of these wandering priests that their stories formed a new mythology. So vast were the real miracles which they were working on men's souls that wonders of a more ordinary sort were assigned to them as a matter of course. They raised the dead, they healed the sick, they cast out devils with a word or with the sign of the cross. Plain facts were too poor for the enthusiasm of German piety; and noble human figures were exhibited, as it were, in the resplendent light of a painted window in the effort to do them exaggerated honour.

It was pity, for truth only smells sweet for ever, and illusions, however innocent, are deadly as the canker-worm. Long cycles had to pass before the fruit of these poison-seeds would ripen. The practical result meanwhile was to substitute in the minds of the sovereign races which were to take the lead in the coming era the principles of the moral law for law of force and the sword.

The Eastern branch of the divided Church experienced meanwhile a less happy fortune. In the East there was no virgin soil like the great noble Teutonic peoples. Asia was a worn-out stage on which drama after drama of history had been played and played out. Languid luxury only was there, huge aggregation of wealth in particular localities, and the no less inevitable shadow attached to luxury by the necessities of things, oppression and misery and squalor. Christianity and the world had come to terms after the established fashion – the world to be let alone in its pleasures and its sins; the Church relegated to opinion, with free liberty to split doctrinal hairs to the end of time. The work of the Church's degradation had begun, even before it accepted the tainted hand of Constantine. Already in the third century speculative Christianity had become the fashionable creed of Alexandria, and had purchased the favour of patrician congregations, if not by tolerance of vice, yet by leaving it to grow unresisted. St Clement details contemptuously the inventory of the boudoir of a fine lady of his flock, the list of essences on her toilet-table, the shoes, sandals, and slippers with which her dainty feet were decorated in endless variety. He describes her as she ascends the steps of the βασιλική, to which she was going for what she called her prayers, with a large page lifting up her train. He paints her as she walks along the street, her petticoats projecting with some horsehair arrangement behind, and the street boys jeering at her as she passes.

All that Christianity was meant to do in making life simple and habit pure was left undone, while, with a few exceptions, like that of St Clement himself, the intellectual energy of its bishops and teachers was exhausted in spinning endless cobwebs of metaphysical theology. Human life at the best is enveloped in darkness; we know not what we are or whither we are bound. Religion is the light by which we are to see our way along the moral pathways without straying into the brake or the morass. We are not to look at religion itself, but at surrounding things with the help of religion. If we fasten our attention upon the light itself, analysing it into its component rays, speculating on the union and composition of the substances of which it is composed, not only will it no longer serve us for a guide, but our dazzled senses lose their natural powers; we should grope our way more safely in conscious blindness.

When the light within you is darkness, how great is that darkness.

In the place of the old material idolatry we erect a new idolatry of words and phrases. Our duty is no longer to be true, and honest, and brave, and self-denying, and pure, but to be exact in our formulas, to hold accurately some nice and curious proposition, to place damnation in straying a hair's breadth from some symbol which exults in being unintelligible, and salvation in the skill with which the mind can balance itself on some intellectual tightrope.

There is no more instructive phenomenon in history than the ease and rapidity with which the Arabian caliphs lopped off the fairest provinces of the Eastern Empire. When nations are easily conquered, we may be sure that they have first lost their moral self-respect. When their religions, as they call them, go down at a breath, those religions have become already but bubbles of vapour. The laws of Heaven are long-enduring, but their patience comes to an end at last. Because justice is not executed speedily men persuade themselves there is no such thing as justice. But the lame foot, as the Greek proverb said, overtakes the swift one in the end; and the longer the forbearance the sharper the retribution when it comes.

As the Greek theology was one of the most complicated accounts ever offered of the nature of God and His relation to man, so the message of Mahomet, when he first unfolded the green banner, was one of the most simple. There is no god but God: God is King, and you must and shall obey His will. This was Islam, as it was first offered at the sword's point to people who had lost the power of understanding any other argument. Your images are wood and stone; your metaphysics are words without understanding; the world lies in wickedness and wretchedness because you have forgotten the statutes of your Master, and you shall go back to those; you shall fulfil the purpose for which you were set to live upon the earth, or you shall not live at all.

Tremendous inroad upon the liberties of conscience! What right, it is asked, have those people that you have been calling soldiers of the Almighty to interfere by force with the opinions of others? Let them leave us alone; we meddle not with them. Let them, if they please, obey those laws they talk of; we have other notions of such things; we will obey ours, and let the result judge between us. The result was judging between them. The meek Apostle with no weapon but his word and his example, and winning victories by himself submitting to be killed, is a fairer object than a fierce Kaled, calling himself the sword of the Almighty. But we cannot order for ourselves in what way these things shall be. The caitiff Damascenes to whom Kaled gave the alternative of the Koran or death were men themselves, who had hands to hold a sword with if they had heart to use it, or a creed for which they cared to risk their lives. In such a quarrel superior strength and courage are the signs of the presence of a nobler conviction.

To the question, 'What right have you to interfere with us?' there is in exceptional times of convulsion but one answer: 'We must. These things which we tell you are true; and in your hearts you know it; your own cowardice convicts you. The moral laws of your Maker are written in your consciences as well as in ours. If you disobey them you bring disaster not only on your own wretched selves, but on all around you. It is our common concern, and if you will not submit, in the name of our Master we will compel you.'

Any fanatic, it will be said, might use the same language. Is not history full of instances of dreamers or impostors, 'boasting themselves to be somebody.' Who for some wild illusion, or for their own ambition, have thrown the world into convulsions? Is not Mahomet himself a signal – the most signal – illustration of it? I should say rather that when men have risen in arms for a false cause the event has proved it by the cause coming to nothing. The world is not so constituted that courage, and strength, and endurance, and organization, and success long sustained are to be obtained in the service of falsehood. If I could think that, I should lose the most convincing reason for believing that we are governed by a moral power. The moral laws of our being execute themselves through the instrumentality of men; and in those great movements which determine the moral condition of many nations through many centuries, the stronger side, it seems to me, has uniformly been the better side, and stronger because it has been better.

I am not upholding Mahomet as if he had been a perfect man, or the Koran as a second Bible. The crescent was no sun, nor even a complete moon reigning full-orbed in the night heaven. The light there was in it was but reflected from the sacred books of the Jews and the Arab traditions. The morality of it was defective. The detailed conception of man's duties inferior, far inferior, to what St Martin and St Patrick, St Columba and St Augustine were teaching or had taught in Western Europe. Mahometanism rapidly degenerated. The first caliphs stood far above Saladin. The descent from Saladin to a modern Moslem despot is like a fall over a precipice. All established things, nations, constitutions, all established things which have life in them, have also the seeds of death. They grow, they have their day of usefulness, they decay and pass away, 'lest one good custom should corrupt the world.'

But the light which there was in the Moslem creed was real. It taught the omnipotence and omnipresence of one eternal Spirit, the Maker and Ruler of all things, by whose everlasting purpose all things were, and whose will all things must obey; and this central truth, to which later experience and broader knowledge can add nothing; it has taught so clearly and so simply that in Islam there has been no room for heresy, and scarcely for schism.

The Koran has been accused of countenancing sensual vice. Rather it bridled and brought within limits a sensuality which before was unbounded. It forbade and has absolutely extinguished, wherever Islam is professed, the bestial drunkenness which is the disgrace of our Christian English and Scottish towns. Even now, after centuries of decay, the Mussulman probably governs his life by the Koran more accurately than most Christians obey the Sermon on the Mount or the Ten Commandments. In our own India, where the Moslem creed retains its relative superiority to the superstitions of the native races, the Mussulman is a higher order of being. Were the English to withdraw he would retake the sovereignty of the peninsula by natural right – not because he has larger bones or sinews, but by superiority of intellect and heart; in other words, because he has a truer faith.

I said that while Christianity degenerated in the East with extreme rapidity, in the West it retained its firmer character. It became the vitalizing spirit of a new organization of society. All that we call modern civilization in a sense which deserves the name is the visible expression of the transforming power of the Gospel.

I said also that by the side of the healthy influences of regeneration there were sown along with it the germs of evil to come. All living ideas, from the necessity of things, take up into their constitutions whatever forces are already working round them. The most ardent aspirations after truth will not anticipate knowledge, and the errors of the imagination become consecrated as surely as the purest impulses of conscience. So long as the laws of the physical world remain a mystery, the action of all uncomprehended phenomena, the movement of the heavenly bodies, the winds and storms, famines, murrains, and human epidemics, are ascribed to the voluntary interference of supernatural beings. The belief in witches and fairies, in spells and talismans, could not be dispelled by science, for science did not exist. The Church therefore entered into competition with her evil rivals on their own ground. The saint came into the field against the enchanters. The powers of charms and amulets were eclipsed by martyrs' relics, sacraments, and holy water. The magician, with the devil at his back, was made to yield to the divine powers imparted to priests by spiritual descent in the impositions of hands.

Thus a gigantic system of supernaturalism overspread the entire Western world. There was no deliberate imposition. The clergy were as ignorant as the people of true relations between natural cause and effect. Their business, so far as they were conscious of their purpose, was to contend against the works of the devil. They saw practically that they were able to convert men from violence and impurity to piety and self-restraint. Their very humility forbade them to attribute such wonderful results to their own teaching. When it was universally believed that human beings could make covenants with Satan by signing their names in blood, what more natural than that they should assume, for instance, that the sprinkling of water, the inaugurating ceremony of the purer and better life, should exert a mysterious mechanical influence upon the character?

If regeneration by baptism, however, with its kindred imaginations, was not true, innocence of intention could not prevent the natural consequences of falsehood. Time went on; knowledge increased; doubt stole in, and with doubt the passionate determination to preserve beliefs at all hazards which had grown too dear to superstition to be parted with. In the twelfth century the mystery called transubstantiation had come to be regarded with widespread misgiving. To encounter scepticism, there then arose for the first time what have been called pious frauds. It was not perceived that men who lend themselves consciously to lies, with however excellent an intention, will become eventually deliberate rogues. The clergy doubtless believed that in the consecration of the elements an invisible change was really and truly effected. But to produce an effect on the secular mind the invisible had to be made visible. A general practice sprung up to pretend that in the breaking of the wafer real blood had gushed out; that real pieces of flesh were found between the fingers. The precious things thus produced were awfully preserved, and with the Pope's blessing were deposited in shrines for the strengthening of faith and the confutation of the presumptuous unbeliever.

When a start has once been made on the road of deception, the after progress is a rapid one. The desired effect was not produced. Incredulity increased. Imposture ran a race with unbelief in the vain hope of silencing inquiry, and with imposture all genuine love for spiritual or moral truth disappeared.

You all know to what condition the Catholic Church had sunk at the beginning of the sixteenth century. An insolent hierarchy, with an army of priests behind them, dominated every country in Europe. The Church was like a hard nutshell round a shrivelled kernel. The priests in parting with their sincerity had lost the control over their own appetites which only sincerity can give. Profligate in their own lives, they extended to the laity the same easy latitude which they asserted for their own conduct. Religious duty no longer consisted in leading a virtuous life, but in purchasing immunity for self-indulgence by one of the thousand remedies which Church officials were ever ready to dispense at an adequate price.

The pleasant arrangement came to an end – a sudden and terrible one. Christianity had not been upon the earth for nothing. The spiritual organization of the Church was corrupt to the core; but in the general awakening of Europe it was impossible to conceal the contrast between the doctrines taught in the Catholic pulpits and the creed of which they were the counterfeit. Again and again the gathering indignation sputtered out to be savagely repressed. At last it pleased Pope Leo, who wanted money to finish St Peter's, to send about spiritual hawkers with wares which were called indulgences – notes to be presented at the gates of purgatory as passports to the easiest places there – and then Luther spoke and the whirlwind burst.

I can but glance at the Reformation in Germany. Luther himself was one of the grandest men that ever lived on earth. Never was any one more loyal to the light that was in him, braver, truer, or wider-minded in the noblest sense of the word. The share of the work which fell to him Luther accomplished most perfectly. But he was exceptional in one way, that in Saxony he had his sovereign on his side, and the enemy, however furious, could not reach him with fleshly weapons, and could but grind his teeth and curse. Other nations who had caught Luther's spirit had to win their liberty on harder terms, and the Catholic churchmen were able to add to their other crimes the cruelty of fiends. Princes and politicians, who had state reasons for disliking popular outbursts, sided with the established spiritual authorities. Heresy was assailed with fire and sword, and a spirit harsher than Luther's was needed to steel the converts' hearts for the trials which came upon them. Lutheranism, when Luther himself was gone, and the thing which England know as Anglicanism, were inclined to temporising and half-measures. The Lutheran congregations were but half-emancipated from superstition, and shrank from pressing the struggle to extremities; and half-measures meant half-heartedness, convictions which were but half-convictions, and truth with an alloy of falsehood. Half-measures, however, would not quench the bonfires of Philip of Spain, or raise men in France or Scotland who would meet crest to crest the Princes of the House of Lorraine. The Reformers required a position more sharply defined, and a sterner leader, and that leader they found in John Calvin.

There is no occasion to say much of Calvin's personal history. His name is now associated only with gloom and austerity. It may be true enough that he rarely laughed. He had none of Luther's genial and sunny humour. Could they have exchanged conditions, Luther's temper might have been somewhat grimmer, but he would never have been entirely like Calvin. Nevertheless, for hard times hard men are needed, and intellects which can pierce to the roots where truth and lies part company. It fares ill with the soldiers of religion when 'the accursed thing' is in their camp. And this is to be said of Calvin, that so far as the state of knowledge permitted, no eye could have detected more keenly the unsound spots in the received creed of the Church, nor was there reformer in Europe so resolute to excise, tear out, and destroy what was distinctly seen to be false – so resolute to establish what was true in its place, and make truth to the last fibre of it in the rule of practical life.

Calvinism as it existed at Geneva, and as it endeavoured to be wherever it took root for a century and a half after him, was not a system of opinion, but an attempt to make the will of God as revealed in the Bible an authoritative guide for social as well as personal direction. Men wonder why the Calvinists, being so doctrinal, yet seem to dwell so much and so emphatically on the Old Testament. It was because in the Old Testament they found, or thought they found, a divine example of national government, a distinct indication of the laws which men were ordered to follow, with visible and immediate punishments attached to disobedience. At Geneva, as for a time in Scotland, moral sins were treated after the example of the Mosaic law, as crimes to be punished by the magistrate. 'Elsewhere,' said Knox, speaking of Geneva, 'the word of God is taught as purely, but never anywhere have I seen God obeyed as faithfully.'

If it was a dream, it was at least a noble one. The Calvinists have been called intolerant. Intolerance of an enemy who is trying to kill you seems to me a pardonable state of mind. It is no easy matter to tolerate lies clearly convicted of being lies under any circumstances; specially it is not easy to tolerate lies which strut about in the name of religion; but there is no reason to suppose that the Calvinists at the beginning would have thought of meddling with the Church if they had been themselves let alone. They would have formed communities apart. Like the Israelites whom they wished to resemble, they would have withdrawn into the wilderness – the Pilgrim Fathers actually did so withdraw into the wilderness of New England – to worship the God of their fathers, and would have left argument and example to work their natural effect. Normal did not kill Cardinal Beaton down in the castle yonder because he was a Catholic, but because he was a murderer. The Catholics chose to add to their already incredible creed a fresh article, that they were entitled to hang and burn those who differed from them; and in this quarrel the Calvinists, Bible in hand, appealed to the God of battles. They grew harsher, fiercer – if you please – more fanatical. It was extremely natural that they should. They dwelt, as pious men are apt to dwell in suffering and sorrow, on the all-disposing power of Providence. Their burden grew lighter as they considered that God had so determined that they must bear it. But they attracted to their ranks almost every man in Western Europe that 'hated a lie.'

They were crushed down, but they rose again. They were splintered and torn, but no power could bend or melt them. They had many faults; let him that is without a sin cast a stone at them. They abhorred as no body of men ever more abhorred all conscious mendacity, all impurity, all moral wrong of every kind so far as they could recognize it. Whatever exists at this moment in England and Scotland of conscientious fear of doing evil is the remnant of the convictions which were branded by the Calvinists into the people's hearts. Though they failed to destroy Romanism, though it survives and may survive as long as an opinion, they drew its fangs; they forced it to abandon that detestable principle, that its was entitled to murder those who dissented from it. Nay, it may be said that by having shamed Romanism out of its practical corruption the Calvinists enabled it to revive.

Why, it is asked, were they so dogmatic? Why could they not be contented to teach men reasonably and quietly that to be wicked and miserable, that in the indulgence of immoderate passions they would find less happiness than in adhering to the rules of justice, or yielding to the impulses of more generous emotions? And, for the rest, why could they not let fools be fools, and leave opinion free about matters of which neither they nor others could know anything certain at all?

I reply that it is not true that goodness is synonymous with happiness. The most perfect being who ever trod the soil of this planet was called the Man of Sorrows. If happiness means the absence of care and inexperience of painful emotion, the best securities for it are a hard heart and a good digestion. If morality has no better foundation than a tendency to promote happiness, its sanction is but a feeble uncertainty. If it be recognized as part of the constitution of the world, it carries with it its right to command; and those who see clearly what it is, will insist on submission to it, and derive authority from the distinctness of their recognition, to enforce submission where their power extends. Philosophy goes no further than probabilities, and in every assertion keeps a doubt in reserve. Compare the remonstrance of the casual passer-by if a mob of ruffians are fighting in the street, with the downright energy of the policeman who strikes in fearlessly, one against a dozen, as a minister of the law. There is the same difference through life between the man who has a sure conviction and him whose thoughts never rise beyond a 'perhaps.'

Every fanatic may say as much, it is again answered, for the wildest madness. But the elementary principles of morality are not forms of madness. No one pretends that it is uncertain whether truth is better than falsehood, or justice than injustice. Speculation can eat away the sanction, superstition can erect rival duties, but neither one nor the other pretends to touch the fact that these principles exist, and the very essence and life of all great religious movements is the recognition of them as of authority and as part of the eternal framework of things.

There is, however, it must be allowed, something in what these objectors say. The power of Calvinism has waned. The discipline which it once aspired to maintain has fallen slack. Desire for ease and self-indulgence drag for ever in quiet times at the heel of noble aspirations, while the shadow struggles to remain and preserve its outline when the substance is passing away. The argumentative and logical side of Calvin's mind has created once more a fatal opportunity for a separation between opinion and morality. We have learnt, as we say, to make the best of both worlds, to take political economy for the rule of our conduct, and to relegate religion into the profession of orthodox doctrines. Systems have been invented to explain the inexplicable. Metaphors have been translated into formulas, and paradoxes intelligible to emotion have been thrust upon the acceptance of the reason; while duty, the loftiest of all sensations which we are permitted to experience, has been resolved into the acceptance of a scheme of salvation for the individual human soul. Was it not written long ago, 'He that will save his soul shall lose it?' If we think of religion only as a means of escaping what we call the wrath to come, we shall not escape it; we are already under it; we are under the burden of death, for we care only for ourselves.

This was not the religion of your fathers; this was not the Calvinism which overthrew spiritual wickedness, and hurled kings from their thrones, and purged England and Scotland, for a time at least, of lies and charlatanry. Calvinism was the spirit which rises in revolt against untruth; the spirit which, as I have shown you, has appeared, and reappeared, and in due time will appear again, unless God be a delusion and man be as the beasts that perish. For it is but the inflashing upon the conscience with overwhelming force of nature and origin of the laws by which mankind are governed – laws which exist, whether we acknowledge them or whether we deny them, and will have their way, to weal or woe, according to the attitude in which we please to place ourselves towards them – inherent, like electricity, in the nature of things, not made by us, not to be altered by us, but to be discerned and obeyed by us at our everlasting peril.

Nay, rather electricity is but a property of material things, and matter and all that belongs to it may one day fade away like a cloud and vanish. The moral law is inherent in eternity. 'Heaven and earth shall pass away, but My word shall not pass away.' The law is the expression of the will of the Spirit of the Universe. The spirit in man which corresponds to and perceives the Eternal Spirit is part of its essence, and immortal as it is immortal. The Calvinists called the eye within us the Inspiration of the Almighty. Aristotle could see that it was not of earth, or any creature of space and time:

ὅ γὰρ νοῦς, (he says) οὐσία τις οὖσα ἔοικεν
ἐγγίγνεσθαι καὶ οὐ φθείρεσθαι.

For the mind, being a substance, seems to be born in us and to be inde-structible.

What the thing is which we call ourselves we know not. It may be true – I for one care not if it be – that the descent of our mortal bodies may be traced through an ascending series to some glutinous organism on the rocks of the primeval ocean. It is nothing to me how the Maker of me has been pleased to construct the perishable frame which I call my body. It is *mine*, but it is not *me*. The νοῦς, the intellectual spirit, being an οὐσία – an essence – we believe to be an incorruptible something which has to be an incorruptible something which has been engendered in us from another source. As Wordsworth says:

Our birth is but a sleep and a forgetting;
The soul that rises with us, our life's star
Hath elsewhere had its setting,
And cometh from afar:
Not in entire forgetfulness,
And not in utter nakedness,
But trailing clouds of glory do we come,
From heaven, which is our home.

Appendix 2

Extract: *The Times of Luther and Erasmus*

The following is an extract from Froude's three lectures on The times of Luther and Erasmus (Short Studies Vol 2). When considering the effects and justification of the Reformation it is essential to bear in mind the nature and tactics of Spain and in particular the Duke of Alba. To understand the pressures both Henry VIII and Elizabeth were under and to appreciate the reasons for their action the facts that Froude puts before us must be taken into account. The picture presented by Robert Hutchinson in his new book, *Henry VIII*, likening him to Stalin, may not be wholly fair.

39

TIMES OF ERASMUS AND LUTHER:

THREE LECTURES

DELIVERED AT NEWCASTLE, 1867.

—◦—

I.

LADIES AND GENTLEMEN,—I do not know whether I have made a very wise selection in the subject which I have chosen for these Lectures. There was a time—a time which, measured by the years of our national life, was not so very long ago—when the serious thoughts of mankind were occupied exclusively by religion and politics. The small knowledge which they possessed of other things was tinctured by their speculative opinions on the relations of heaven and earth ; and, down to the sixteenth century, art, science, scarcely even literature, existed in this country, except as, in some way or other, subordinate to theology. Philosophers—such philosophers as there were—obtained and half deserved the reputation of quacks and conjurers. Astronomy was confused with astrology.

The physician's medicines were supposed to be power-
less, unless the priests said prayers over them. The
great lawyers, the ambassadors, the chief ministers of
state, were generally bishops; even the fighting business was not entirely secular. Half-a-dozen Scotch
prelates were killed at Flodden; and, late in the reign
of Henry the Eighth, no fitter person could be found
than Rowland Lee, Bishop of Coventry, to take command of the Welsh Marches, and harry the freebooters
of Llangollen.

Every single department of intellectual or practical
life was penetrated with the beliefs, or was interwoven
with the interests, of the clergy; and thus it was that,
when differences of religious opinion arose, they split
society to its foundations. The lines of cleavage penetrated everywhere, and there were no subjects whatever
in which those who disagreed in theology possessed any
common concern. When men quarrelled, they quarrelled altogether. The disturbers of settled beliefs were
regarded as public enemies who had placed themselves
beyond the pale of humanity, and were considered fit
only to be destroyed like wild beasts, or trampled out
like the seed of a contagion.

Three centuries have passed over our heads since
the time of which I am speaking, and the world is so
changed that we can hardly recognize it as the same.

The secrets of nature have been opened out to us on
a thousand lines; and men of science of all creeds can
pursue side by side their common investigations. Catholics, Anglicans, Presbyterians, Lutherans, Calvinists,

contend with each other in honourable rivalry in arts, and literature, and commerce, and industry. They read the same books. They study at the same academies. They have seats in the same senates. They preside together on the judicial bench, and carry on, without jar or difference, the ordinary business of the country.

Those who share the same pursuits are drawn in spite of themselves into sympathy and good-will. When they are in harmony in so large a part of their occupations, the points of remaining difference lose their venom. Those who thought they hated each other, unconsciously find themselves friends; and as far as it affects the world at large, the acrimony of controversy has almost disappeared.

Imagine, if you can, a person being now put to death for a speculative theological opinion. You feel at once, that in the most bigoted country in the world such a thing has become impossible; and the impossibility is the measure of the alteration which we have all undergone. The formulas remain as they were on either side—the very same formulas which were once supposed to require these detestable murders. But we have learnt to know each other better. The cords which bind together the brotherhood of mankind are woven of a thousand strands. We do not any more fly apart or become enemies, because, here and there, in one strand out of so many, there are still unsound places.

If I were asked for a distinct proof that Europe was improving and not retrograding, I should find it in this phenomenon. It has not been brought about by controversy. Men are fighting still over the same questions which they began to fight about at the Reformation. Protestant divines have not driven Catholics out of the field, nor Catholics, Protestants. Each polemic writes for his own partisans, and makes no impression on his adversary.

Controversy has kept alive a certain quantity of bitterness; and that, I suspect, is all that it would accomplish if it continued till the day of judgment. I sometimes, in impatient moments, wish the laity in Europe would treat their controversial divines as two gentlemen once treated their seconds, when they found themselves forced into a duel without knowing what they were quarrelling about.

As the principals were being led up to their places, one of them whispered to the other, 'If you will shoot your second, I will shoot mine.'

The reconciliation of parties, if I may use such a word, is no tinkered-up truce, or convenient Interim. It is the healthy, silent, spontaneous growth of a nobler order of conviction, which has conquered our prejudices even before we knew that they were assailed. This better spirit especially is represented in institutions like the present, which acknowledge no differences of creed —which are constructed on the broadest principles of toleration—and which, therefore, as a rule, are wisely protected from the intrusion of discordant subjects.

They exist, as I understand, to draw men together, not to divide them—to enable us to share together in those topics of universal interest and instruction which all can take pleasure in, and which give offence to none.

If you ask me, then, why I am myself departing from a practice which I admit to be so excellent, I fear that I shall give you rather a lame answer. I might say that I know more about the history of the sixteenth century than I know about anything else. I have spent the best years of my life in reading and writing about it; and if I have anything to tell you worth your hearing, it is probably on that subject.

Or, again, I might say—which is indeed most true —that to the Reformation we can trace, indirectly, the best of those very influences which I have been describing. The Reformation broke the theological shackles in which men's minds were fettered. It set them thinking, and so gave birth to science. The reformers also, without knowing what they were about, taught the lesson of religious toleration. They attempted to supersede one set of dogmas by another. They succeeded with half the world—they failed with the other half. In a little while it became apparent that good men—without ceasing to be good—could think differently about theology, and that goodness, therefore, depended on something else than the holding orthodox opinions.

It is not, however, for either of these reasons that I am going to talk to you about Martin Luther: nor is toleration of differences of opinion, however excellent it be, the point on which I shall dwell in these Lectures.

Were the Reformation a question merely of opinion,

I for one should not have meddled with it, either here or anywhere. I hold that, on the obscure mysteries of faith, every one should be allowed to believe according to his conscience, and that arguments on such matters are either impertinent or useless.

But the Reformation, gentlemen, beyond the region of opinions, was a historical fact—an objective something which may be studied like any of the facts of nature. The Reformers were men of note and distinction, who played a great part for good or evil on the stage of the world. If we except the Apostles, no body of human beings ever printed so deep a mark into the organization of society; and if there be any value or meaning in history at all, the lives, the actions, the characters of such men as these can be matters of indifference to none of us.

We have not to do with a story which is buried in obscure antiquity. The facts admit of being learnt. The truth, whatever it was, concerns us all equally. If the divisions created by that great convulsion are ever to be obliterated, it will be when we have learnt, each of us, to see the thing as it really was, and not rather some mythical or imaginative version of the thing— such as from our own point of view we like to think it was. Fiction in such matters may be convenient for our immediate theories, but it is certain to avenge itself in the end. We may make our own opinions, but facts were made for us; and if we evade or deny them, it will be the worse for us.

Unfortunately, the mythical version at present very

largely preponderates. Open a Protestant history of
the Reformation, and you will find a picture of the
world given over to a lying tyranny—the Christian
population of Europe enslaved by a corrupt and degraded priesthood, and the Reformers, with the Bible
in their hands, coming to the rescue like angels of light.
All is black on one side—all is fair and beautiful on the
other.

Turn to a Catholic history of the same events and
the same men, and we have before us the Church of the
Saints fulfilling quietly its blessed mission in the saving
of human souls. Satan a second time enters into Para-
dise, and a second time with fatal success tempts miserable man to his ruin. He disbelieves his appointed
teachers, he aspires after forbidden knowledge, and at
once anarchy breaks loose. The seamless robe of the
Saviour is rent in pieces, and the earth becomes the
habitation of fiends.

Each side tells the story as it prefers to have it;
facts, characters, circumstances, are melted in the
theological crucible, and cast in moulds diametrically
opposite. Nothing remains the same except the names
and dates. Each side chooses its own witnesses.
Everything is credible which makes for what it calls
the truth. Everything is made false which will not fit
into its place. 'Blasphemous fables' is the usual
expression in Protestant controversial books for the
accounts given by Catholics. 'Protestant tradition,'
says an eminent modern Catholic, 'is based on lying—
bold, wholesale, unscrupulous lying.'

Now, depend upon it, there is some human account of the matter different from both these if we could only get at it, and it will be an excellent thing for the world when that human account can be made out. I am not so presumptuous as to suppose that I can give it to you; still less can you expect me to try to do so within the compass of two or three lectures. If I cannot do everything, however, I believe I can do a little; at any rate I can give you a sketch, such as you may place moderate confidence in, of the state of the Church as it was before the Reformation began. I will not expose myself more than I can help to the censure of the divine who was so hard on Protestant tradition. Most of what I shall have to say to you this evening will be taken from the admissions of Catholics themselves, or from official records earlier than the outbreak of the controversy, when there was no temptation to pervert the truth.

Here, obviously, is the first point on which we require accurate information. If all was going on well, the Reformers really and truly told innumerable lies, and deserve all the reprobation which we can give them. If all was not going on well—if, so far from being well, the Church was so corrupt that Europe could bear with it no longer—then clearly a Reformation was necessary of some kind; and we have taken one step towards a fair estimate of the persons concerned in it.

A fair estimate—that, and only that, is what we want. I need hardly observe to you, that opinion in England has been undergoing lately a very considerable alteration about these persons.

Two generations ago, the leading Reformers were looked upon as little less than saints; now a party has risen up who intend, as they frankly tell us, to un-Protestantize the Church of England, who detest Protestantism as a kind of infidelity, who desire simply to reverse everything which the Reformers did.

One of these gentlemen, a clergyman writing lately of Luther, called him a heretic, a heretic fit only to be ranked with—whom, do you think?—Joe Smith, the Mormon Prophet. Joe Smith and Luther—that is the combination with which we are now presented.

The book in which this remarkable statement appeared was presented by two bishops to the Upper House of Convocation. It was received with gracious acknowledgments by the Archbishop of Canterbury, and was placed solemnly in the library of reference, for that learned body to consult.

So, too, a professor at Oxford, the other day, spoke of Luther as a Philistine—a Philistine meaning an oppressor of the chosen people; the enemy of men of culture, and intelligence, such as the professor himself.

One notices these things, not as of much importance in themselves, but as showing which way the stream is running; and, curiously enough, in quite another direction we may see the same phenomenon. Our liberal philosophers, men of high literary power and reputation, looking into the history of Luther, and Calvin, and John Knox, and the rest, find them falling far short of the philosophic ideal—wanting sadly in many qualities which the liberal mind cannot dispense with.   They are discovered to be intolerant, dogmatic, narrow-minded, inclined to persecute Catholics as Catholics had persecuted them; to be, in fact, little if at all better than the popes and cardinals whom they were fighting against.

Lord Macaulay can hardly find epithets strong enough to express his contempt for Archbishop Cranmer. Mr Buckle places Cranmer by the side of Bonner, and hesitates which of the two characters is the more detestable.

An unfavourable estimate of the Reformers, whether just or unjust, is unquestionably gaining ground among our advanced thinkers. A greater man than either Macaulay or Buckle—the German poet, Goethe—says of Luther, that he threw back the intellectual progress of mankind for centuries, by calling in the passions of the multitude to decide on subjects which ought to have been left to the learned. Goethe, in saying this, was alluding especially to Erasmus. Goethe thought that Erasmus, and men like Erasmus, had struck upon the right track; and if they could have retained the direction of the mind of Europe, there would have been more truth, and less falsehood, among us at this present time. The party hatreds, the theological rivalries, the persecutions, the civil wars, the religious animosities which have so long distracted us, would have been all avoided, and the mind of mankind would have expanded gradually and equably with the growth of knowledge.

Such an opinion, coming from so great a man, is not to be lightly passed over. It will be my endeavour to show you what kind of man Erasmus was, what he was aiming at, what he was doing, and how Luther spoilt his work—if spoiling is the word which we are to use for it.

One caution, however, I must in fairness give you before we proceed further. It lies upon the face of the story, that the Reformers imperfectly understood toleration; but you must keep before you the spirit and temper of the men with whom they had to deal. For themselves, when the movement began, they aimed at nothing but liberty to think and speak their own way. They never dreamt of interfering with others, although they were quite aware that others, when they could, were likely to interfere with them. Lord Macaulay might have remembered that Cranmer was working all his life with the prospect of being burnt alive as his reward—and, as we all know, he actually was burnt alive.

When the Protestant teaching began first to spread in the Netherlands—before one single Catholic had been ill-treated there, before a symptom of a mutinous disposition had shown itself among the people, an edict was issued by the authorities for the suppression of the new opinions.

The terms of this edict I will briefly describe to you.

The inhabitants of the United Provinces were informed that they were to hold and believe the doctrines of the Holy Roman Catholic Church. 'Men and women,' says the edict, 'who disobey this command shall be punished as disturbers of public order. Women who have fallen into heresy shall be buried alive. Men, if they recant, shall lose their heads. If they continue obstinate, they shall be burnt at the stake.

'If man or woman be suspected of heresy, no one shall shelter or protect him or her; and no stranger shall be admitted to lodge in any inn or dwelling-house unless he bring with him a testimonial of orthodoxy from the priest of his parish.

'The Inquisition shall inquire into the private opinions of every person, of whatever degree; and all officers of all kinds shall assist the Inquisition at their peril. Those who know where heretics are concealed, shall denounce them, or they shall suffer as heretics themselves. Heretics (observe the malignity of this paragraph)—heretics who will give up other heretics to justice, shall themselves be pardoned if they will promise to conform for the future.'

Under this edict, in the Netherlands alone, more than fifty thousand human beings, first and last, were deliberately murdered. And, gentlemen, I must say that proceedings of this kind explain and go far to excuse the subsequent intolerance of Protestants.

Intolerance, Mr Gibbon tells us, is a greater crime in a Protestant than a Catholic. Criminal intolerance, as I understand it, is the intolerance of such an edict as that which I have read to you—the unprovoked intolerance of difference of opinion. I conceive that the most enlightened philosopher might have grown hard and narrow-minded if he had suffered under the administration of the Duke of Alva.

Dismissing these considerations, I will now go on with my subject.

Never in all their history, in ancient times or modern, never that we know of, have mankind thrown out of themselves anything so grand, so useful, so beautiful, as the Catholic Church once was. In these times of ours, well-regulated selfishness is the recognized rule of action—every one of us is expected to look out first for himself, and take care of his own interests. At the time I speak of, the Church ruled the State with the authority of a conscience; and self-interest, as a motive of action, was only named to be abhorred. The bishops and clergy were regarded freely and simply as the immediate ministers of the Almighty; and they seem to me to have really deserved that high estimate of their character. It was not for the doctrines which they taught only, or chiefly, that they were held in honour. Brave men do not fall down before their fellow-mortals for the words which they speak, or for the rites which they perform. Wisdom, justice, self-denial, nobleness, purity, highmindedness,—these are the qualities before which the free-born races of Europe have been contented to bow; and in no order of men were such qualities to be found as they were found six hundred years ago in the clergy of the Catholic Church. They called themselves the successors of the Apostles. They claimed in their Master's name universal spiritual authority, but they made good their pretensions by the holiness of their own lives. They were allowed to rule because they deserved to rule, and in the fulness of re-

verence kings and nobles bent before a power which
was nearer to God than their own.   Over prince and
subject, chieftain and serf, a body of unarmed defence-
less men reigned supreme by the magic of sanctity.
They tamed the fiery northern warriors who had broken
in pieces the Roman Empire.   They taught them—
they brought them really and truly to believe—that
they had immortal souls, and that they would one day
stand at the awful judgment bar and give account for
their lives there.   With the brave, the honest, and the
good—with those who had not oppressed the poor nor
removed their neighbour's landmark—with those who
had been just in all their dealings—with those who had
fought against evil, and had tried valiantly to do their
Master's will,—at that great day, it would be well.
For cowards, for profligates, for those who lived for
luxury and pleasure and self-indulgence, there was the
blackness of eternal death.

An awful conviction of this tremendous kind the
clergy had effectually instilled into the mind of Europe.
It was not a PERHAPS; it was a certainty.   It was not
a form of words repeated once a week at church; it
was an assurance entertained on all days and in all
places, without any particle of doubt.   And the effect
of such a belief on life and conscience was simply im-
measurable.

I do not pretend that the clergy were perfect.
They were very far from perfect at the best of times,
and the European nations were never completely sub-
missive to them.   It would not have been well if they

had been. The business of human creatures in this planet is not summed up in the most excellent of priestly catechisms. The world and its concerns continued to interest men, though priests insisted on their nothingness. They could not prevent kings from quarrelling with each other. They could not hinder disputed successions, and civil feuds, and wars, and political conspiracies. What they did do was to shelter the weak from the strong.

In the eyes of the clergy, the serf and his lord stood on the common level of sinful humanity. Into their ranks high birth was no passport. They were themselves for the most part children of the people; and the son of the artisan or peasant rose to the mitre and the triple crown, just as now-a-days the rail-splitter and the tailor become Presidents of the Republic of the West.

The Church was essentially democratic, while at the same time it had the monopoly of learning; and all the secular power fell to it which learning, combined with sanctity and assisted by superstition, can bestow.

The privileges of the clergy were extraordinary. They were not amenable to the common laws of the land. While they governed the laity, the laity had no power over them. From the throne downwards, every secular office was dependent on the Church. No king was a lawful sovereign till the Church placed the crown upon his head: and what the Church bestowed, the Church claimed the right to take away. The disposition of property was in their hands. No will

could be proved except before the bishop or his officer;
and no will was held valid if the testator died out of
communion. There were magistrates and courts of
law for the offences of the laity. If a priest committed
a crime, he was a sacred person. The civil power
could not touch him; he was reserved for his ordinary.
Bishops' commissaries sat in town and city, taking
cognizance of the moral conduct of every man and
woman. Offences against life and property were tried
here in England, as now, by the common law; but the
Church Courts dealt with sins—sins of word or act. If
a man was a profligate or a drunkard; if he lied or
swore; if he did not come to communion, or held
unlawful opinions; if he was idle or unthrifty; if he
was unkind to his wife or his servants; if a child was
disobedient to his father, or a father cruel to his child;
if a tradesman sold adulterated wares, or used false
measures or dishonest weights,—the eye of the parish
priest was everywhere, and the Church Court stood
always open to examine and to punish.

Imagine what a tremendous power this must have
been! Yet it existed generally in Catholic Europe
down to the eve of the Reformation. It could never
have established itself at all unless at one time it had
worked beneficially—as the abuse of it was one of the
most fatal causes of the Church's fall.

Extract: *Condition and Prospects of Protestantism*

⸺⸺◇⸺⸺

IN one of the western counties, the writer of this paper was recently present at an evening Evangelical prayer-meeting. The congregation were partly church-goers, partly dissenters of various denominations, united for the time by the still active revivalist excitement. Some were highly educated men and women: farmers, tradesmen, servants, sailors, and fishermen made up the rest: all were representative specimens of Evangelical Christians, passionate doctrinalists, convinced that they, and only they, possessed the 'Open Sesame' of heaven, but doing credit to their faith by inoffensive, if not useful, lives. One of them, who took a leading part in the proceedings, was a person of large fortune, who was devoting his money, time, and talents to what he called the truth. Another was well known through two counties as a hard-headed, shrewd, effective man of business; a stern, but on the whole, and as times went, beneficent despot over many thousands of unmanageable people.

The services consisted of a series of addresses from different speakers, interchanged with extempore prayers, directed rather to the audience than to the Deity. At intervals, the congregation sung hymns, and sung them particularly well. The teaching was of the ordinary kind expressed only with more than usual distinctness. We were told that the business of each individual man and woman in the world was to save his or her soul; that we were all sinners together—all equally guilty, hopeless, lost, accursed children, unable to stir a finger or do a thing to help ourselves. Happily, we were not required to stir a finger; rather, we were forbidden to attempt it. An antidote had been provided for our sins, and a substitute for our obedience. Everything had been done for us. We had but to lay hold of the perfect righteousness which had been fulfilled in our behalf. We had but to put on the vesture provided for our wearing, and our safety was assured. The reproaches of conscience were silenced. We were perfectly happy in this world, and certain to be blessed in the next. If, on the other hand, we neglected the offered grace; if, through carelessness, or intellectual perverseness, or any other cause, we did not apprehend it in the proper manner; if we tried to please God ourselves by 'works of righteousness,' the sacrifice would then cease to avail us. It mattered nothing whether, in the common acceptation of the word, we were good or bad; we were lost all the same, condemned by perfect justice to everlasting torture.

It is, of course, impossible for human creatures to

act towards one another on these principles.   The man of business on week days deals with those whom he employs on week-day rules.   He gives them work to do, and he expects them to do it.   He knows the meaning of good desert as well as of ill desert.   He promises and he threatens.   He praises and he blames. He will not hear of vicarious labour.   He rewards the honest and industrious.   He punishes the lazy and the vicious.   He finds society so constructed that it cannot exist unless men treat one another as responsible for their actions, and as able to do right as well as wrong.

And, again, one remembered that the Christian's life on earth used to be represented as a warfare ; that the soldier who went into battle considering only how he could save his own life, would do little credit to the cause he was fighting for ; and that there were other things besides and before saving their souls which earnest men used to think about.

The listeners, however, seemed delighted.   They were hearing what they had come to hear—what they had heard a thousand times before, and would hear with equal ardour a thousand times again—the gospel in a nutshell ; the magic formulas which would cheat the devil of his due.   However antinomian the theory might sound, it was not abused by anybody present for purposes of self-indulgence.   While they said that it was impossible for men to lead good lives, they were, most of them, contradicting their words by their practice.   While they professed to be thinking only of their personal salvation, they were benevolent, generous, and self-forgetful. People may express themselves in what formulas they please; but if they sincerely believe in God, they try to act uprightly and justly; and the language of theology, hovering, as it generally does, between extravagance and conventionality, must not be scanned too narrowly.

There is, indeed, attaching to all propositions, one important condition—that they are either true or false; and it is noticeable that religious people reveal unconsciously, in their way of speaking, a misgiving that the ground is insecure under them. We do not mean, of course, that they knowingly maintain what they believe may possibly be a mistake; but whatever persuasion they belong to, they do not talk about truth, but they talk about *the truth; the truth* being the doctrine which, for various reasons, they each prefer. Truth exists independently of them. It is searched for by observation and reason. It is tested by evidence. There is a more and a less in the degree to which men are able to arrive at it. On the other hand, for *the truth* the believer has the testimony of his heart. It suits his spiritual instincts; it answers his spiritual desires. There is no 'perhaps' about it; no balancing of argument. Catholics, Anglicans, Protestants are each absolutely certain that they are right. God, it would seem, makes truth; men make *the truth;* which, more or less, approaches to the other, but is not identical with it. If it were not so, these different bodies, instead of quarrelling, would agree. The measure of

approximation is the measure of the strength or usefulness of the different systems.   Experience is the test.
If in virtue of any creed men lead active, upright,
self-denying lives, the creed itself is tolerable ; and
whatever its rivals may say about it, is not, and cannot
be, utterly false.

It seems, however, as if the Evangelicals were pain-
fully anxious to disclaim any such criterion.   When
the first address was over, the congregation sung the
following singular hymn, one of a collection of which,
it appeared from the title-page, that many hundred
thousand copies were in circulation :

> Nothing, either great or small,
>   Nothing, sinners, no ;
> Jesus did it—did it all
>   Long, long ago.
>
> It is finished, yes, indeed,
>   Finished every jot :
> Sinners, this is all you need,
>   Tell me, Is it not ?
>
> When He from His lofty throne
>   Stooped to do and die,
> Everything was fully done :
>   Hearken to His cry,—
>
> Weary, weary, burdened one,
>   Wherefore toil you so ?
> Cease your doing, all was done
>   Long, long ago.
>
> Till to Jesus' work you cling
>   By a simple faith,
> Doing is a deadly thing,
>   Doing ends in death.
>
> Cast your deadly doing down,
>   Down at Jesus' feet,

Stand in Him, in Him alone,
Gloriously complete.

And this, we said to ourselves, is Protestantism. To do our duty has become a deadly thing. This is what, after three centuries, the creed of Knox and Luther, of Coligny and Gustavus Adolphus, has come to. The first Reformers were so anxious about what man did, that if they could they would have laid the world under a discipline as severe as that of the Roman Censors. Their modern representatives are wiser than their fathers and know better what their Maker requires of them. To the question, 'What shall I do to inherit eternal life?' the answer of old was not, 'Do nothing,' but 'Keep the commandments.' It was said by the Apostle from whose passionate metaphors Protestant theology is chiefly constructed, that 'the Gentiles, who did by nature the things contained in the law,' were on the road to the right place. But we have changed all that. We are left face to face with a creed which tells us that God has created us without the power to keep the commandments,—that He does not require us to keep them; yet at the same time that we are infinitely guilty in His eyes for not keeping them, and that we justly deserve to be tortured for ever and ever, to suffer, as we once heard an amiable excellent clergyman express it, ' to suffer the utmost pain which Omnipotence can inflict, and the creature can endure, without annihilation.'

The scene of the evening was too soothing at the time for unpleasant reflections on the paradoxes of

theology. The earnest attention, the piety, the evident
warmth of belief, the certainty that those who were so
loudly denouncing the worth of human endeavour
would carry away with them a more ardent desire to do
the works of righteousness of which they were denying
the necessity—these things suggested happier conclusions on the condition of humanity : when the hearts of
men are sound, the Power which made and guides us
corrects the follies of our heads.

Nevertheless, when we are considering the general
influence for good or evil of a system or systems, the
intellectual aspect of them cannot be disregarded. Religion is, or ought to be, the consecration of the whole
man, of his heart, his conduct, his knowledge, and his
mind, of the highest faculties which have been given in
trust to him, and the highest acquirements which he
has obtained for himself. When the gospel was first
made generally known through the Roman Empire, it
attracted and absorbed the most gifted and thoughtful
men then living. Pagan philosophy of the post-Chris-
tian era has left no names which will compete on its
own ground with those of Origen, Tertullian, and
Clement of Alexandria. When the Reformers broke
the spell of superstition in the sixteenth century, their
revolt was ascribed by the Catholics to the pride of
human reason. Some enchantment must now have
passed over Protestantism, or over the minds of those
to whom it addresses itself, when science and cultivation are falling off from it as fast as Protestantism fell
away from its rival. How has a creed which had once

sounded the spiritual reveillé like the blast of the arch-
angel's trumpet come now to proclaim in passionate
childishness the 'deadliness' of human duty?

The best that every man knows dies with him; the
part of him which he can leave behind in written words
conveys but half his meaning even to the generation
which lies nearest to him, to the men whose minds are
under the same influences with his own. Later ages,
when they imagine that they are following the thoughts
of their forefathers, are reading their own thoughts
in expressions which serve to them but as a mirror.
The pale shadow called Evangelical religion clothes
itself in the language of Luther and Calvin. Yet what
Luther and Calvin meant is not what it means. The
Protestantism of the sixteenth century commanded the
allegiance of statesmen, soldiers, philosophers, and men
of science. Wherever there was a man of powerful
intelligence and noble heart, there was a champion of
the Reformation: and the result was a revival, not of
internal emotion, but of moral austerity. The passion
of Evangelical teachers in every country where the
Reformation made its way, was to establish, so far as
the world would let them, the discipline of Geneva, to
make men virtuous in spite of themselves, and to treat
sins as crimes. The writings of Knox and Latimer
are not more distinguished by the emphasis with which
they thunder against injustice and profligacy than by
their all but total silence on 'schemes of salvation.'
The Protestantism of the nineteenth century has for-
saken practice for opinion.

Appendix 4

A Cardinal, a King and a Saint

I recently came across the actual text of three sermons preached by Bishop Clemens von Galen in Münster Cathedral in 1941. I vaguely remembering hearing about him as a schoolboy at the time and about how his stand helped to convince us that it was wrong to think, as was often said at the time, that 'the only good German was a dead one'. His sermons now seem to me to be a remarkable illustration not only of some of the main points of Froude's views on religion, but also of how heroic good can come out of the most terrible and destructive evil. They reminded me especially of what Froude said at the beginning of the Short Study on Calvinism: 'systems of religion have been vigorous and effective precisely to the extent to which they may have seen in the existing order of things the hand of a Living Ruler.' A passage from one of those sermons shows exactly this:

> At this present time we are the anvil not the hammer. Remain steadfast and firm like the anvil receiving all the blows that rain down on us, in loyal service to our people and country, but also ready at any time to act, in the spirit of supreme sacrifice, in accordance with the precept: 'Men must obey God more than men.' Through a conscience formed by faith God speaks to each one of us. Obey always without doubt the voice of conscience.

Take as your model the old Prussian minister of justice – I have spoken of him before – who was ordered by King Frederick the Great to overturn and alter in accordance with the monarch's wishes a judgment which he had pronounced in accordance with the law. Then this true nobleman, a certain Herr von Munchhausen, gave his king this magnificent answer; 'My head is at your majesty's disposal, but not my conscience.' Thus he wanted to say I am ready to die for my king; indeed I am obedient to him and shall even accept death at the hands of the hangman. My life belongs to the king, not my conscience, that belongs to God! Is this race of noblemen, who have this attitude and act in accordance with it, are Prussian officials of this stamp now extinct? Are there no longer any citizens or country people, craftsmen or workers of similar mind? That I cannot and will not believe.. And so I say once again; become hard, remain firm, remain steadfast! Like the anvil under the blows of the hammer! It may be that obedience to our God and faithfulness to our conscience may cost me or any of you life, freedom or home. But: 'better to die than to sin!' May the grace of God, without which we can do nothing, grant this unshakable firmness to you and to me and keep us in it!'

Martin Luther would not have quarrelled with this. In fact he justified his own actions precisely on these grounds. Further the Bishop was well aware that his message was directed to more than just Catholics as is shown by the following passage:

I shall forbear to mention any other names today. The name of a Protestant minister who served Germany in the first world war as a German officer and a submarine commander, who later worked as a Protestant minister in Munster and for some years now has been deprived of his liberty, is well known to you, and we all have the greatest respect for this noble German's courage and steadfast-ness in professing his faith. From this example you will see that I am not talking about a matter of purely Catholic concern but about a matter of Christian concern, indeed of general human and national concern. 'Justice is the foundation of all states!' We lament, we observe with the greatest anxiety that this foundation is now shaken, that justice – the natural and Christian virtue which is indispensable for the ordered existence of any human community – is no longer maintained and held in honour in a for everybody unequivocally recognisable way... No holder of authority can expect to command the loyalty and willing service of honourable men unless his actions and penal decisions prove in an impartial judgment to be free of any element of arbitrariness and weighed on the incorruptible scales of justice. Accordingly the practice of condemning men who are given no chance of defence and without any judicial sentence, ... engenders a feeling of legal defencelessness and an attitude of apprehensive timidity and subservient cowardice, which must in the long run deprave the national character and destroy the national community.'

Bishop von Galen does not hesitate to give concrete examples of what is happening, which he says must be opposed not by revolution but by determined resistance:

One of the patients in Marienthal [mental hospital] was a man of 55, a farmer from a country parish in the Munster region – I could give you his name – who has suffered for some years from mental disturbance and was therefore admitted to Marienthal hospital. He was not mentally ill in the full sense, he could receive visits and was always happy when his relatives came to see him. Only a fortnight ago he was visited by his wife and one of his sons, a soldier on leave from the front. The son is much attached to his father, and the parting was a sad one: no one can tell whether the soldier will return to see his father again, since he may fall in battle for his country. The son, the soldier, will certainly never again see his father on earth, for he has since then been put on the list of the 'unproductive'. A relative, who wanted to visit the father this week in Marienthal, was turned away with the information that the patient had been transferred elsewhere on the instructions of the Council of State for National Defence. No information could be given about where he had been sent, but the relatives would be informed within a few days. What information will they be given? The same as in other cases of the kind? That the man has died, that his body has been cremated, that his ashes will be handed over on the payment of a fee? The soldier risking his life in the field for his fellow-countrymen, will not see his father again on earth, because his fellow-countrymen at home have killed him.'

Bishop von Galen rams his point home by saying that if some official committee is to decide who is unproductive and must therefore be killed , woe betide us all when we grow old and unproductive. The bishop himself laid his own life on the line.

Martin Bormann wanted him taken into custody and hanged but Hitler feared that it would mean the loss of the support of the whole diocese of Munster for the duration of the war. It was on grounds of very similar injustices that Froude attacked the edict of the Inquisition. Certainly in circumstances such as these the integrity of noble, true and honest men and women shines out, whereas in a milder political climate it is much harder to oppose the rottenness that little by little takes root in their communities.

Nietzsche feared that when we oppose monsters we are in danger of becoming like them ourselves. Of course the Western World is not like Hitler's Europe but a pale shadow hangs over it. There is a tendency to water down what Bishop von Galen calls 'the natural and Christian virtue which is indispensable for the ordered existence of any human community. Justice,' he says, ' is the foundation of all states.' There has been a glorification of youth in our pop culture and that has blurred some of the wiser tendencies of our traditional culture and a degree of dishonesty in our politics that sometimes only just holds back from some of the flagrant injustices of the Nazis.

Another frightening example of the hand of a living ruler in history is to be found in St. Augustine's *City of God*, a book which he wrote when the Roman Empire was collapsing around him and which he might have thought had no hope of being influential. And yet it survived for hundreds of years through the Dark Ages in the cloisters of monasteries, finally to give birth to the civilisation of small states of the Middle Ages. Augustine was answering those who blamed the catastrophe of Rome's downfall on Christianity.

> Were your famous Scipio Nasica, once your pontiff, still living - who was unanimously chosen by the Senate when the best man was required, and appointed to take up the sacred objects from Phrygia during the panic of the Carthaginian war, a man whom perhaps you would hardly dare to look in the face – even he would hold you back from impudence like this. Why , when afflicted by adversities, do you complain against the Christian era unless because you wish to maintain your luxury untroubled and to abandon yourselves to the most damnable practices with no harsh

touch of vexing problems? For your desire for peace and abundant wealth of every sort does not spring from any intention of enjoying these boons in a respectable way, that is, decently, soberly, temperately, devoutly. Rather you would use them to procure an infinite variety in your unwholesome dissipations; you would engender in times of prosperity a moral plague of ills worse than raging enemies.

That Scipio, your chief pontiff, the best man of all in the judgment of the whole Senate, because he feared that calamity, refused to agree to the destruction of Rome's rival for empire, Carthage, and said the opposite of Cato, who advised its destruction. For he feared security as the enemy of unstable minds and saw that fear was indispensable to the citizens to serve as it were, as guardian of their immaturity.

In this opinion he was not mistaken, for the outcome showed how truly he spoke. Of course, once Carthage was destroyed, which meant that the great bugbear of the Roman Republic had been beaten off and annihilated these mighty evils sprang up as a sequel to prosperity. First, harmony was crumpled and breached in the fierce and bloody strife of parties. Next, there followed, by a chain of evil causes, civil wars, which brought such massacres, so much bloodshed. Such effervescence of cruelty induced by the craving for proscriptions and plunder, that those Romans who, when life had more integrity, feared the evils enemies might bring, now when that integrity of living went by the board, suffered greater cruelties from fellow citizens. Finally, that passion for rule which among the other vices of mankind was found more concentrated in the Roman people one and all, when it had won victory in the case of a few more dominating men, subjected the others worn out and tired, to the yoke of slavery.

A similar phenomenon occurred in towns in the USA in the last century where its inhabitants lived a fairly hard life but were relatively kindly to each other, who suddenly, when oil was found, turned into cauldrons of vicious rivalry. What is clear from this is that all three men, Froude, von Galen and Augustine, saw in existing conditions the hand of a living ruler. So it is also clear that peace and prosperity, so perpetually claimed as the aim of our modern society, even to the extent of going to war to ensure that others have it, is not necessarily the best condition for human well-being. The production of too many material goods may not only damage the environment, but cause men to fight over them and enrich excessively 'a few more dominating men'.

What that well-being consists in is not always obvious. Francis Bacon, in the *Advancement of Learning*, advises: 'Let the mind be enlarged, according to its capacity, to the grandeur of the mysteries, and not the mysteries contracted to the narrowness of the mind.' Genetic theory appears to have established that there is a pattern of life stretching through the ages on which our present manifestation of life is dependent. Is it too fanciful to suggest that there might be some kind of storehouse below the level of consciousness in which our responses to life, in particular our responses to persecution and abuse, such as those of men like the Bishop who lived with their lives under threat, are stored? Otherwise how can such noble self-sacrifice make any kind of sense and who would not say that it represented the power of Right over Might?

Bibliography

J.A Froude *Oceana* New Edition 1886

J.A Froude *Short Studies on Great Subjects* Vols 1 and 2 Longmans, Green and Co. London 1872

J.A Froude *The Earl of Beaconsfield* Dent 1905 (Republished as *Disraeli - a Biography* New European Publications 2004)

W.H Dunn *James Anthony Froude - a Biography 1857-1894* Clarendon Press, Oxford 1963

Leopold Kohr *The Breakdown of Nations* Green books 2001

Richard Body *The Breakdown of Europe* New European Publications 1998

E.F Schumacher *Small is Beautiful* Blond and Briggs 1973

Richard Body *England for the English* New European Publications 2001

St Augustine *City of God* Loeb Classical Library Harvard 2003

Aidan Rankin *The Politics if the Forked Tongue* New European Publications 2002

Andrew Roberts *Salisbury - Victorian Titan* Weidenfelt and Nicolson 1999

M Gayford, D Kindersley, L.L Cardozo Kindersley *Apprenticeship* The Cardozo Kindersley Workshop

William James *The Varieties of Religious Experience* Penguin 2003

Robert Hutchinson *Henry VIII* Weidenfield and Nicholson 2005

An interesting account of the Catholic Church working beneficially is to be found in Bertrand Russell's *History of Western Philosophy* in the Chapter entitled 'Three Doctors of the Church'.

Notes

Chapter 1
1. J.A Froude *Oceana*
2. *Politics of the Forked Tongue* Aidan Rankin
3. Emeka Anyaoku, *New European Vol 5 No 1 – Europe or the Commonwealth – a False Dichotomy*
4. John Biggs-Davison, *New European Vol 1 No 3 – The Two Commonwealths, Continental and Oceanic*
5. John Coleman, Salisbury Review Vol 21 No 1 2002
6. Waldo Hilary Dunn *James Anthony Froude*
7. Ibid
8. J.A Froude *The Earl of Beaconsfield*
9. J.A Froude *Short Studies on Great Subjects* Vol 2 England her Colonies
10. W.H Dunn *James Anthony Froude – a Biography*
11. Ibid
12. Ibid
13. Ibid
14. Andrew Roberts *Salisbury – Victorian Titan*
15. John Ruskin *Sesame and Lilies* Dent 1907

Chapter 2
1. J.A Froude *Short Studies Vol 2* Education – Inaugural Address
2. Ibid
3. Ibid
4. Ibid

5. Ibid
6. Ibid
7. Ibid
8. Ibid
9. Ibid
10. Ibid
11. Ibid
12. Ibid
13. Ibid
14. Ibid
15. Ibid
16. Ibid
17. Ibid
18. Ibid
19. Ibid
20. W.H Dunn *James Anthony Froude – a Biography*

Chapter 3

1. J.A Froude *Short Studies* Vol 2 Calvinism
2. Ibid
3. Ibid
4. Ibid
5. Ibid
6. Richard Ingrams *The Observer* 30 May 2004
7. J.A Froude *Short Studies*
8. Ibid
9. Prince of Wales quoted in *Apprenticeship – the Necessity of Learning by Doing*

Chapter 4

1. W.H Dunn *James Anthony Froude – a Biography*
2. Ibid
3. J.A Froude *The Earl of Beaconsfield*
4. W.H Dunn *James Anthony Froude – a Biography*
5. Ibid

Chapter 5

1. J.A Froude *Short Studies* Vol 2 England and Her Colonies
2. Ibid
3. Ibid Scientific Method Applied to History
4. W.H Dunn *James Anthony Froude – a Biography*

5. Ibid
6. J.A Froude *Short Studies* Vol 2 England's War
7. Ibid Fortnight in Kerry
8. W.H Dunn *James Anthony Froude – a Biography*
9. J.A Froude *Oceana*
10. W.H Dunn *James Anthony Froude – a Biography*

Chapter 6
1. W.H Dunn *James Anthony Froude* Vol 2
2. William Dwight Witney *Who are the Americans?* Eyre and Spottiswoode
3. Trevor Lloyd-Hughes *The Times* 23 February 2000
4. Richard Body *England for the English*
5. W.H Dunn *James Anthony Froude* Vol 2

Chapter 7
1. Leopold Kohr *The Breakdown of Nations*
2. The Cobden speech was delivered in Rochdale on 29th October, 1862

Index